Freedom From Overthinking in Relationships

*Escape Anxiety and Doubt, Rewire Your Mind,
and Finally Feel Safe, Secure, and Deeply Connected in Love*

MARIA ELAINA PASWELL

© **Copyright 2024 - All rights reserved.**

The content contained within this book may not be reproduced, duplicated, or transmitted without direct written permission from the author or the publisher.

Under no circumstances will any blame or legal responsibility be held against the publisher or author for any damages, reparation, or monetary loss due to the information contained within this book, either directly or indirectly.

Legal Notice:

This book is copyright protected and is only for personal use. You cannot amend, distribute, sell, use, quote, or paraphrase any part of the content within this book without the consent of the author or publisher.

Disclaimer Notice:

Please note the information contained within this document is for educational and entertainment purposes only. All efforts have been executed to present accurate, up-to-date, reliable, and complete information. No warranties of any kind are declared or implied. Readers acknowledge that the author is not engaged in the rendering of legal, financial, medical, or professional advice. The content within this book has been derived from various sources. Please consult a licensed professional before attempting any techniques outlined in this book.

By reading this document, the reader agrees that under no circumstances is the author responsible for any losses, direct or indirect, that are incurred as a result of the use of the information contained within this document, including, but not limited to, errors, omissions, or inaccuracies.

Table of Contents

Introduction 9

ℛ: **Recognizing the Root Causes and Triggers of Your Overthinking Habit** 13

1. What It Means to Overthink—How It Affects Your Relationships 15

What Does It Mean to Overthink? 15

Signs of Overthinking 17

Causes of Overthinking 19

Is Overthinking a Mental Disorder? 21

Types of Overthinking 22

What Is the Difference Between Overthinking and Problem-Solving? 23

What Is the Difference Between Anxiety and Overthinking? 25

The Impact of Overthinking on Your Life: How Overthinking Affects Your Life 26

Mental health 27

Relationships 28

Physical Health 29

Exercise 29

2. The Path to Self-Awareness—Uncovering Patterns and Triggers 31

The Importance of Self-Awareness in Emotional Intelligence 31

Self-Awareness Archetypes 32

How Increasing Self-Awareness Can Help You Conquer Overthinking in Your Relationship 33

Why is self-awareness vital in relationships? 34

How a Lack of Self-Awareness in Relationships Can Destroy the Relationship 35

Identifying Triggers 36

Understanding Emotions: Gaining a Deeper Understanding of Your Emotional Responses in Relationships 38

Understanding Your Emotions 39

The Key Elements of Emotions 40

Emotional Suppression 42

Managing Your Emotions 42

Managing As They Come 43

How to Increase Self-Awareness With Your Partner 44

Exercise 46

Reflection questions: 46

3. Rewiring Negative Thoughts to End Self-Sabotage 49

What Are Cognitive Distortions? 49

Causes and Triggers 50

How Cognitive Distortions Impact Your Well-Being...51

How Cognitive Distortions Result in Self-Sabotage in Relationships...................52

Causes of Self-Sabotaging in Relationships 53

Nine Cognitive Distortions That Can Lead to Overthinking
and Self-Sabotage in Your Relationships 55

How to Stop Self-Sabotaging in Relationships 57

How Do You Identify and Manage Cognitive Distortions?.....................................58

Exercise 60

Part 1: Identify Your Cognitive Distortions..60

Part 2: Reflection on Your Distortions..60

Part 3: Questioning Your Thoughts..61

&: **Engaging in Self-Care Practices and Improving Relationship Quality**.. 63

4. The Path to a Calm and Anxiety-Free Relationship 65

How Stress and Anxiety Can Lead to Overthinking and Vice Versa 65

What Is Relationship Anxiety? 67

Roots of Relationship Anxiety...68

Indicators of Relationship Anxiety...69

Impact of Relationship Anxiety 71

Overcoming Relationship Anxiety 72

Signs That Stress Is Affecting Your Relationship 73

How to Deal With Relationship Stress 75

Exercise 76

5. Embracing the Beauty of Imperfection in Relationships 81
Understanding Perfectionism 81
Causes 83
Types of Perfectionism 85
Traits and Symptoms 86
Perfectionism and Its Impact 87
Characteristics of Perfectionism in Relationships 88
How to Overcome Perfectionism in Relationships 90
How Perfectionism Can Cause Anxiety 91
How to Stop Anxiety Intruding on Decisions 93
Exercise 94
Mid-Book Reflection: Share Your Thoughts 97

6. Unlocking Trust: The Secrets to Building a Healthy, Strong Bond 99
What Are Trust Issues? 99
What Causes Trust Issues? 100
Types of Trust Issues in a Relationship 102
What Are the Signs of Trust Issues? 103
Benefits of Trust 105
How to Overcome Trust Issues in Your Relationship 107
Exercise 108

7. Investing in Your Relationship to Achieve Emotional Balance 111
Emotional Investment 111
Things to Consider Before Investing Your Emotions Into a Relationship 112
How to Strengthen Your Relationship With Your Partner 114

Emotional Bank Account 115

How to Invest in Your Emotional Bank Account 117

Maintain a Positive Balance in Your Emotional Bank Account 118

Making Deposits 119

Minimizing Withdrawals 120

Key Messages 121

Why Some People Are Afraid to Invest Their Emotions in a Relationship 122

How to Recognize a One-Sided Relationship and Restore the Balance 124

Common Signs of Imbalance 125

Are One-Sided Relationships Worth Fixing? 126

What About a Partner Who Does Not Want to Change? 127

How to End Things 128

Exercise 130

S: Securing Your Identity 133

8. Elevating Your Self-Worth by Building Confidence and Esteem 135

The Difference Between Self-Confidence and Self-Esteem 135

How Low Self-Confidence and Self-Esteem Can Lead to Overthinking 136

Signs You Have Low Self-Esteem and Self-Confidence 137

Low Self-Esteem 137

Low Confidence 138

Causes of Low Self-Confidence and Low Self-Esteem 138

How to Build Self-Confidence and Self-Esteem 140

How Do You Build Self-Esteem and Confidence in a Relationship? 142

Exercise 144

Part 7: Tailoring Your Communication Approach 147

9. Empathy, Active Listening, and Vulnerability—Keys to Healthy Communication 149

How Poor Communication Can Lead to Overthinking and Vice Versa 149

What Constitutes Poor Communication 151

Good Communication in a Relationship 153

Signs a Relationship Has Healthy Communication 155

Things That Can Inhibit Good Communication 156

The Importance of Emotional Awareness in Communication 157

How to Communicate Better in a Relationship to Stop Overthinking 158

What to Do When Your Partner Is a Poor Communicator 159

Seven Active Listening Techniques 160

Exercise 161

Conclusion 165

Thank You for Coming on This Journey 167

References 169

Introduction

Anna, a young woman with a sharp mind, has always been a thinker. Even as a child, she would analyze every word spoken to her, and every glance exchanged, searching for hidden meanings. Growing up in a household where attention was scarce and affection even rarer, Anna's overthinking became a shield—a way to anticipate the unpredictable and protect herself from potential hurt. This pattern persisted into her adult life, especially in her romantic relationships. Simple misunderstandings became complex tangles of doubts, and every quiet moment reminded her of her worries.

One day, during a casual conversation at a local gathering, Anna met Sarah. As they shared stories, Sarah's journey sounded eerily familiar. Like Anna, Sarah had faced a childhood marked by neglect. However, unlike Anna, Sarah had found a way to break free from the shackles of overthinking. As Anna listened to Sarah's story, she began to grasp that there could be a way around her spiraling thoughts. She recognized that Sarah's real change came from addressing the root causes of her overthinking, not just managing the symptoms. It was a revelation for Anna: Perhaps she, too, could find a way to change her patterns to forge healthier, happier relationships.

If you find yourself continuously engaged in a web of overthinking, particularly about your relationships, you are not alone. I understand the crushing weight of worry, the fear of vulnerability, and the never-ending self-doubt that haunts your thoughts. My name is Maria Elaina Paswell, and I have committed my life to supporting others like you on their journeys of self-improvement and emotional well-being.

This book was born from the realization that many people may face similar challenges. It recognizes and tackles the stress and anxiety that comes with analyzing your partner's every word and action, the fear of relying on someone else, the pursuit of perfection, and the difficulties that arise in maintaining effective communication.

You deserve to be at ease in your relationships, especially romantic ones. It is time to release ourselves from the chains of overthinking and uncover the road to making healthy connections. As a counselor and life coach with over two decades of experience, I created the R.E.S.T. Approach. This roadmap will assist you through the transformation process.

The R.E.S.T. Approach is not just an acronym; it's a foundation for reclaiming control over your thoughts and emotions:

R—Recognize the root causes and triggers of your overthinking habit, empowering you to make radical changes.

E—Engage in self-care practices and improve relationship quality, managing stress and anxiety while overcoming perfectionism.

S—Secure your identity by boosting self-confidence and self-esteem, ensuring you recognize your worth.

T—Tailor your communication approach, allowing you to express concerns clearly and prevent assumptions about your relationship.

Throughout this journey, be patient and kind to yourself. Embrace the baby steps, knowing that progress and growth take time, trial, and error. Together, let us begin this transformative journey to overcome anxiety and self-doubt, build confidence, and create meaningful, authentic connections through vulnerable communication.

Recognizing the Root Causes and Triggers of Your Overthinking Habit

1.
What It Means to Overthink— How It Affects Your Relationships

Life is a series of constantly changing moments, like negative and positive thoughts. Although it may be human nature to dwell, like many natural things, it is senseless to allow a single thought to inhabit a mind because thoughts are like guests or fair-weather friends.

–Cecelia Ahern

What Does It Mean to Overthink?

Overthinking is like a tangled web your mind weaves, trapping you in a loop of thoughts that never seem to end. It's that late-night session when your brain decides to replay every awkward conversation you have ever had or that moment when you are trying to make a simple decision but end up contemplating every possible outcome.

It's like a mental marathon, with your thoughts racing in every direction possible, making it nearly impossible to find peace of mind.

The misconception that overthinking leads to better solutions is like a hamster running on a wheel—lots of effort but no progress. The more you dwell on a problem, the less energy you have to confront it directly. It's like trying to drive with the parking brake on—exhausting yourself without moving forward.

Overthinking can be sneaky. It starts with a minor concern or a harmless thought, and before you know it, your mind is caught in a spider's web of hypotheticals. What if I had handled it differently? What if they don't approve of me? What if everything goes awry? It's a mental labyrinth that seems impossible to escape.

The process of overthinking involves analyzing situations from various angles and anticipating potential outcomes. While it may feel like you are preparing for every possibility, it can also lead to anxiety, stress, and even depression.

Imagine your mind as a busy highway with thoughts racing by. Overthinking is like a traffic jam—everything comes to a screeching halt as your mind fixates on one particular issue. This gridlock prevents you from moving forward, hindering your ability to focus on other aspects of your life.

Recognizing the signs of overthinking is crucial. Are you caught in a cycle of repetitive thoughts, imagining the worst, or replaying past events like a broken record? These are the red flags signaling that overthinking has taken the wheel.

Breaking free from the detrimental habit of overthinking requires a deliberate and conscious effort. Instead of getting stuck in a cycle of endless pondering, it's essential to take a step back and ask yourself: What practical steps can I take to address this situation? You can take concrete actions to tackle the issue by identifying feasible and reasonable solutions. It's crucial to redirect your thoughts toward constructive paths rather than letting them linger on the negative aspects.

Overthinking is a common struggle that most people have experienced at some point. It's important to recognize and acknowledge this tendency, but it's equally vital to actively work towards breaking free from its grip. Don't allow your mind to become a breeding ground for unnecessary stress and anxiety. While life presents various challenges, the key lies in confronting them directly instead of becoming entangled in the complex web of overthinking.

Signs of Overthinking

1. Ruminating thoughts: Continuously fixating on the same ideas, anxieties, or fears can lead to a cycle of over-analysis. For instance, spending hours replaying a conversation in your mind, analyzing every word and gesture.

2. Worst-case scenario imagining: Habitually imagining the worst possible scenarios or potential disasters in different situations. For example, before going on a trip, you might catch yourself thinking about all the things that could go wrong, like missing a flight or losing luggage, creating a mental image of the journey turning into a complete disaster.

3. Replaying past incidents: Spending nights fixating on a missed opportunity, replaying the scenario, and thinking of various ways you could have handled it differently is an example of recurrently

replaying anything terrible or unfortunate that occurred in the past and refusing to let it go.

4. Negative future thoughts: Excessive time spent thinking about negative future scenarios can lead to increased worry. For instance, if you're considering a new career path, constantly worrying about potential obstacles such as fear of failure or financial challenges can create uncertainty, making it difficult to take the first step toward a fulfilling and rewarding future.

5. Emotional impact: Feeling unhappy due to continuous unpleasant thoughts. For example, consistently feeling down, dwelling on thoughts of not being good enough, or wishing aspects of your life were different can lead to dissatisfaction and unhappiness.

6. Difficulty concentrating: Having difficulty concentrating on responsibilities due to an overwhelming fixation on a specific idea or problem. For example, being unable to focus at work due to constant preoccupation with a personal worry.

7. Failure to move on: Continuing to ruminate on a situation long after identifying potential solutions, finding it challenging to release it from your thoughts. For instance, persisting in holding onto a disagreement with a friend, repeatedly replaying the scenario in your mind, and constructing new assumptions despite having already addressed and resolved the issue.

8. Inability to progress: Being unable to shift focus to the next important matter due to ongoing rumination on a single problem. For example, stalling on a work project because you cannot stop thinking about a minor issue that occurred earlier in the day.

Causes of Overthinking

We have all been caught up in overthinking, that common source of stress and frustration. Whether lost in future worries, stuck in past ruminations, or overly critical of others, our knack for deep thinking sometimes plays tricks on us. However, before we dive into how to kick the habit of overthinking, let us unravel why we tend to get stuck in this loop.

1. Early life lessons: Many of us who cannot shake off overthinking got into the habit way back when we were kids. It was not for no reason—it was often a way to handle scary or challenging situations. For instance, growing up with an alcoholic parent might have made us pros at obsessively worrying about what could go wrong when they came home. The thing is, what got us into overthinking back then might not be the same thing keeping us there now, even though our brain might be tricked into thinking that it is.

2. The need for control: Who enjoys feeling helpless? None of us! This is especially true when it comes to our loved ones. We all want to help when someone close is going through a tough time. However, the reality is that we can only do so much. Instead of facing this helplessness, many of us deny it and, as a result, start overthinking. Although thinking might feel like we are doing something, giving us a sense of control, it's not always helpful. The problem is that the long-term costs usually outweigh that feeling—chronic anxiety, low self-esteem, and relentless stress.

3. The comfort of certainty: We all struggle with uncertainty. We prefer to feel sure about how things will turn out, especially when a lot is at stake. To avoid the uncomfortable feeling of not knowing, we sometimes convince ourselves that things are more predictable than they actually are. Overthinking becomes a way to stay

in problem-solving mode, making us believe there is a solution to every problem if we think hard enough. However, reality is often much more uncertain than we want to admit. Facing up to uncertainty is the real challenge.

4. Chasing perfection: Perfectionism is not about reaching flawlessness; it's about striving to feel flawless. If you struggle with perfectionism, you may find it difficult to move on from tasks because they don't meet your standards of perfection—whether it's a blog post, a report, or a piano piece you want to perform flawlessly. The truth is, you don't actually believe that you need to be perfect because you know it's impossible. However, you can't handle feeling anything less than perfect. So, what do you do? You tend to overthink, using distractions to avoid feeling inadequate and imperfect (Wignall, 2021). If this resonates with you, it's essential to start working on tolerating the feeling of not being perfect.

5. Hidden rewards: Some people continue to overthink because it has hidden benefits. It can lead to receiving sympathy and pity from others, providing an emotional boost. It may also serve as an excuse for procrastination. If you convince yourself you haven't thought enough, you can't be blamed for a bad decision. If you are overthinking, it's likely because you perceive some gain from it. Breaking the cycle of overthinking involves finding less stressful ways to obtain those same benefits.

6. Overgeneralization: For some of us, thinking is a tool we use expertly in certain areas of life, like work or school. But here's the catch: We are so good at it and get rewarded for it that we need help putting that tool down in other areas where it could be more helpful. You know the saying, "To a hammer, everything looks like a nail"? To the expert thinker, everything starts looking like

a problem to be solved with lots of thinking. If you are an overthinker, list different parts of your life and ask if more thinking is the best way to handle them.

7. Fear of shake-ups: Who enjoys conflict? Most of us avoid it when we can, so we don't get much practice handling it well. That lack of practice makes us less confident in dealing with conflict in the future, leading to even more avoidance. It is a cycle that keeps on going. But here's the thing: Avoiding conflict doesn't make it less scary. Treating all conflicts as dangerous means, you spend a lot of mental energy figuring out how to dodge even the most minor disagreements. It is time to rethink that approach.

Understanding why we overthink is the first step in breaking free from the cycle. By addressing these relatable causes, we can develop healthier ways to cope, reduce stress, and regain control over our thoughts and actions. After all, we are all in this together!

Is Overthinking a Mental Disorder?

Overthinking itself is not officially recognized as a distinct mental disorder. However, research indicates that it often emerges as a symptom of other mental health conditions, including depression, anxiety disorders, obsessive-compulsive disorder (OCD), and posttraumatic stress disorder (PTSD).

While there is no specific diagnosis for an "overthinking disorder," it is crucial to note that overthinking can be linked to broader psychological conditions. Generalized anxiety disorder, for instance, often involves persistent worry and excessive self-reflection, which can manifest as overthinking. Other conditions, such as body dysmorphia or social anxiety disorder, may also contribute to repetitive and intrusive thoughts.

While overthinking per se does not have a dedicated diagnostic category, it is essential to recognize when it significantly impacts mental health. Seeking help is crucial, especially if symptoms of other psychological conditions accompany overthinking. Taking proactive steps to address these concerns can lead to better mental well-being.

Types of Overthinking

Experts do not categorize overthinking into specific "types." However, some people tend to overthink through what they call cognitive distortions—essentially, ways of thinking that often bring on stress, anxiety, and even depression.

- All-or-nothing thinking: Ever catch yourself seeing situations only in black or white? This is all-or-nothing thinking. Instead of recognizing both the positive and negative aspects of an event, you might find yourself analyzing it as either a total success or a complete failure. Life is rarely that straightforward, right?

- Catastrophizing: Picture this—you are worried about failing an exam, and suddenly, your mind spirals into a series of worst-case scenarios. You fear failing the class, which then turns into failing school, not getting a degree, and, naturally, ending up jobless. Catastrophizing tends to make us stress about overly dramatic worst-case outcomes that are often far from reality.

- Overgeneralizing: Imagine building a rule or expectation for the future based on a single or random event from the past. Instead of recognizing that different outcomes are possible, you might start assuming that things will "always" or "never" happen in a certain way. Overgeneralizing leads to unnecessary worry about events that might never actually occur.

- Jumping to conclusions: Two ways to jump to conclusions are mind reading and fortune telling. Mind reading involves thinking someone will react in a particular way or assuming they are thinking things they are not. Fortune telling means predicting events will unfold in a specific way, often to avoid facing a challenging task. A simple solution? Pause, consider the facts, ask questions, and challenge your initial assumptions.

- Emotional reasoning: Have you ever judged yourself or your circumstances based solely on your emotions? That's called emotional reasoning. It means assuming that if you're feeling a negative emotion, it accurately reflects reality. For example, feeling guilty might lead to the conclusion that you're a terrible person. Emotional reasoning is common in people dealing with anxiety and depression. Still, many of us fall into this way of thinking. Cognitive behavior therapy can help you realize that feelings are not always facts.

If you catch yourself falling into these overthinking patterns, know that you're not alone—many of us experience these mental twists and turns.

What Is the Difference Between Overthinking and Problem-Solving?

When problem-solving, we seek solutions by taking action, using strategies, and refining our skills. This proactive approach reduces stress and brings a sense of accomplishment.

On the other hand, overthinking involves excessively dwelling on problems through rumination and analysis rather than focusing on finding a resolution. Unfortunately, this tendency to overthink only amplifies distress, leading to heightened anxiety and a perpetual state of unease.

It is easy to confuse overthinking with creative problem-solving, as our brains naturally enjoy the challenge of finding solutions. However, it is crucial to recognize the distinction between the two.

Operating on autopilot, our brains have a penchant for creating problems and dramas, sometimes subconsciously. This could be a mechanism to experience the pleasure of problem-solving or shielding ourselves from potential pain. Many individuals find themselves stuck in the loop of overthinking, cycling through similar and repetitive thoughts without progress (Astahov Skis, 2022).

Consider this: When we overthink, we become trapped in a cycle of pondering solutions without genuinely intending to solve the problem. We are stuck because our brains resist halting the "problem-solving" process. The danger lies in believing that constant mental activity is valuable. It takes courage and self-awareness to distinguish between overthinking and productive problem-solving.

Participating in brainstorming sessions to explore various solutions proves beneficial when facing challenges. Overthinking, however, often leads to rumination, which keeps you stuck in an unending thought loop without a conclusion. To break out from this cycle, concentrate on the parts of the situation you have control over while learning to let go of the rest. Extended periods of overthinking will not offer you the peace and satisfaction you want. Instead, recognize when you are overthinking, occupy yourself, and then return to the problem more constructively. Finding a balance between addressing issues and avoiding the trap of overthinking is critical.

What Is the Difference Between Anxiety and Overthinking?

It is pretty common for people dealing with anxiety to get caught up in their thoughts. However, not everyone who overthinks is necessarily dealing with anxiety. They are similar but not the same. Let's explore how they can coexist in certain situations.

Example 1: Emily loves her job, but these days, she cannot shake the feeling that she is not measuring up. Every interaction at work repeats in her mind, making her worry that her colleagues do not appreciate her efforts. This constant mental replay leads to nights without sleep and a sense of unease. Emily's overthinking is fueled by this fear of not meeting expectations, even though she objectively does a great job.

In Emily's case, anxiety is a prominent factor, encompassing feelings of fear, unease, and persistent thoughts about work. Her tendency to overthink is intensified, almost like it's on steroids, fueled by the fear of falling short of expectations.

Example 2: Jake is currently in full planning mode for a surprise anniversary celebration for his partner. He is overflowing with excitement and is deeply immersed in daydreams about creating the perfect evening. Although he is overthinking every detail, it comes from pure joy and anticipation, not anxiety or fear.

In Jake's world, the concept of overthinking is characterized by an emphasis on positive vibes and the anticipation of something truly remarkable. While there exists the potential for it to transition into a state of anxiety, at present, it is solely focused on the exhilaration of crafting an unforgettable and meaningful experience.

Moreover, here is a little side note: Anxiety often brings along physical symptoms like sweating and a racing heart. On the flip side, overthinking might not appear in your body, but it can leave you mentally wiped out.

If you're struggling with anxiety or overthinking, it's a good idea to seek help from a mental health professional. It's essential to understand the difference between the two in order to address them effectively. Anxiety, characterized by fear and uneasiness, may require medication or therapy to alleviate the worry. On the other hand, overthinking is more of a habit and can be changed with conscious effort. Cognitive-behavioral therapy (CBT) helps identify and challenge the negative thoughts that drive overthinking.

The journey towards managing anxiety and overthinking involves gaining a deep understanding of these challenges, learning practical strategies to manage them, and discovering healthier ways to navigate through difficult moments.

The Impact of Overthinking on Your Life: How Overthinking Affects Your Life

When your mind becomes trapped in a relentless loop of overthinking, it feels like being caught in a never-ending whirlwind of thoughts and worries. We all experience moments when we overanalyze things, but when it transforms into hours of obsessing over the most minor details, it can significantly disrupt your inner peace and emotional well-being. Overthinking doesn't just remain confined to your thoughts; it affects how you interact with the world around you, making it more challenging to make decisions, be fully present in the moment, and effectively manage everyday stressors. This persistent cycle of overthinking can profoundly impact various aspects of your life, from your relationships to your overall sense of contentment and fulfillment.

Mental health

The toll overthinking takes on your mental health is no joke. These thought patterns can negatively impact your psychological and physical well-being, whether caught up in past mistakes or worrying about what is coming next. Studies even show that dwelling on stress can lead to anxiety and depression over time (McCallum, 2021).

Now, let's dive into some real-life scenarios:

- Spiraling: This is when thoughts or emotions follow a repetitive and intensifying pattern, creating a mental loop that can lead to heightened anxiety or emotional distress. It involves a deepening and escalating cycle that may be challenging to break.

- From overthinking to anxiety: Overthinking and anxiety go hand in hand; dissecting past and future events breeds anxiety, triggering racing thoughts, pounding heart, and stress hormones, impacting mental health and possibly leading to Generalized Anxiety Disorder (GAD).

- From overthinking to depression: The relentless cycle of negative thoughts and perceived failures leads to feelings of hopelessness and low self-esteem, which are common symptoms of depression. It feels like being trapped in a complex mental maze, making it difficult to find a way out and affecting overall mental well-being.

- Decision-making dilemma: Constantly second-guessing oneself makes even simple choices paralyzing. This indecisiveness leads to frustration and a sense of helplessness, contributing further to mental distress.

- The pursuit of perfection paradox: Striving for perfection requires a relentless focus on every detail, no matter how small, and a continuous commitment to identifying and rectifying any mistakes that may arise along the way. Overthinkers may have overly high expectations, resulting in persistent stress and self-criticism.

Relationships

A relationship becomes challenging for someone who overthinks, imagining worst-case scenarios that end in partner desertion, cheating, or even planning harm. Overthinking in relationships is not gender-specific; it affects both men and women.

- Worst-case assumptions: Overthinkers assume the worst, creating unnecessary stress. Constantly assuming the worst can lead to psychological responses, derailing the quality of the relationship.

- There is no good enough reason: Overthinkers can argue endlessly without a valid reason, aware that it is detrimental but unable to stop the cycle.

- Irrational behavior: Overthinking clouds rationality, putting partners and families under extreme stress. Overthinkers constantly fear worst-case scenarios, impacting their loved ones.

- Becoming too suspicious: Overthinkers become overly suspicious, checking phones and creating a distrustful environment. They are aware of the harmful signs but struggle to break the cycle.

- Your imagination runs wild: Overthinking leads to creating mountains out of molehills, causing panic and stress. The fertile imagination can sometimes lead to overthinking and ultimately sabotage relationships.

Physical Health

If left unchecked, overthinking has the potential to become a daily habit. Failing to take proactive steps to manage it affects your emotional well-being and poses a risk to your physical health.

- High blood pressure: Constant overthinking steals peace of mind, inviting stress that can raise blood pressure, making individuals susceptible to heart problems.

- Sleep problems: Overthinkers often have trouble sleeping, leading to fatigue, decreased productivity, and potential weight gain.

- Suppresses appetite: Overthinking can disrupt eating habits, leading to loss of appetite or overeating, both of which are harmful to health.

- Impacts the brain: Changes in brain structure and connectivity due to overthinking can lead to mood disorders and mental illnesses, affecting focus, problem-solving, and decision-making.

- Affects the digestive system: Stress from overthinking can adversely impact digestive health, leading to gastrointestinal problems such as inflammatory bowel disease (IBD) or irritable bowel syndrome (IBS).

Exercise

Embarking on a journey of self-reflection is a powerful step toward understanding the nuances of your relationship. These questions delve into the core of your connection, offering an opportunity to unravel what is working, what needs attention, and the underlying dynamics shaping your journey together. Take some time with your journey and explore each question in detail.

1. Do you share complete trust?
2. Do soul mates resonate with you, and do you see it in each other?
3. When did "I love you" last cross your lips, and why the delay?
4. Is the intimacy satisfying?
5. How frequent are shared laughs?
6. Are personal sacrifices reciprocated?
7. Does thinking of your partner bring a smile?
8. Does attraction from others trigger threats, and why?
9. Is your partner your biggest advocate?
10. How do you feel about financial views?

As you navigate these reflective questions, remember there are no definitive answers— only insights. Trust the authenticity of your responses and the growth they may inspire. Seeking clarity within yourself lays the foundation for fostering a deeper connection and understanding in your relationship.

In exploring overthinking, we realize that comprehension is merely the initial step. To effectively overcome the intricacies of this mental pattern, it is essential to embark on a profound journey of self-awareness. This involves a comprehensive investigation into our thoughts, emotions, and behaviors, delving into the underlying causes and triggers of overthinking. This introspective process will be thoroughly examined in the upcoming chapter, where we will delve into practical strategies and techniques for enhancing self-awareness and managing overthinking tendencies.

2.
The Path to Self-Awareness—Uncovering Patterns and Triggers

*Strong people have a strong sense of self-worth and self-awareness;
they do not need the approval of others.*

–Roy T. Bennett

The Importance of Self-Awareness in Emotional Intelligence

Self-awareness is the ability to tune in to our actions, thoughts, and emotions, assessing how they align with our inner compass. When deeply self-aware, you are not just navigating; you are orchestrating—objectively evaluating, steering your emotions, and ensuring your behavior resonates with your values. It is not about perfection but about knowing how others perceive you and creating genuine connections.

In simpler terms, being highly self-aware lets us interpret our actions, feelings, and thoughts. This skill is a rare gem in a world where emotions often take the lead. Cultivating self-awareness is like giving yourself the superpower to reassess, adapt, and grow, especially for leaders charting their course through challenges.

- Internal awareness: This involves understanding your thoughts, feelings, and emotions—unraveling the patterns and motives shaping your actions.

- External awareness: On the other hand, this is about grasping how your behavior and emotions ripple through the lives of others. It is a dance of understanding, acknowledging the impact you wield in your interactions.

In the grand artistry of personal growth, self-awareness is a companion helping us navigate the complexities of our hearts and the hearts of those around us.

Self-Awareness Archetypes

Understanding self-awareness involves recognizing four types, each characterizing a distinct balance between internal and external self-awareness:

1. Introspectors: These individuals possess high internal self-awareness but struggle with the external dimension. Deeply reflective introspectors gain a profound understanding of who they are through introspection. However, they might shy away from challenging their own views or seeking external feedback.

2. Seekers: On the opposite end, Seekers grapple with both internal and external self-awareness. Uncertain about their identity and how others perceive them, seekers may experience stagnation

and frustration in relationships and performance. Their journey involves navigating the nuanced balance of self-discovery and understanding their impact on the external world.

3. The Aware: Those falling into this archetype strike a harmonious balance with high internal and external self-awareness. They comprehend their identity and goals and actively seek and value external perspectives. Leaders embodying The Aware archetype fully grasp the profound benefits of self-awareness, recognizing the synergy between internal authenticity and external insights.

4. Pleasers: On the other hand, exhibit low internal but high external self-awareness. They prioritize external perception, often at the expense of their internal authenticity. Immersed in concerns about how they come across, Pleasers may overlook their true values and identity. This tendency can lead to decisions that compromise personal success and self-worth.

Understanding these self-awareness archetypes offers a valuable compass for personal growth, emphasizing the importance of balancing internal clarity with external insights. Whether you resonate with introspection, seek external validation, find equilibrium, or lean toward people-pleasing, the journey toward self-awareness is a dynamic exploration.

How Increasing Self-Awareness Can Help You Conquer Overthinking in Your Relationship

Self-awareness in the context of relationships is like having a trustworthy map; it does not make the journey flawless but makes it easier to navigate. No one has an ultimate manual for understanding oneself, but being aware of your own talents, weaknesses, and quirks is like having a key to better relationships.

No one expects you to know exactly who you are. Everyone has blind spots. However, even a small amount of self-awareness can significantly improve relationship skills and mental well-being. It is not a major accomplishment; it's like having a practical tool for dealing with daily challenges, especially overthinking.

Why is self-awareness vital in relationships?

Primarily, your happiness forms the bedrock of a robust partnership. Redirecting focus inward, rather than fixating on your partner's actions, fosters personal growth. It entails assuming responsibility for your well-being, discovering inner joy, and infusing positivity into the relationship.

It also helps you recognize patterns. You know those couples who seem to replay the same arguments on a loop? With self-awareness, you become your own detective. It is about looking back, understanding your role in past mistakes, and choosing a different approach for a better outcome.

Last but not least, let's talk about empathy. When you are aware of your own thoughts and feelings, you become more in tune with others. It is like having a sixth sense of understanding emotions, making communicating, setting boundaries, and creating a more open and loving connection easier.

In a nutshell, it is about being aware of your own steps and how they shape the journey. Embracing your quirks and imperfections is the foundation for building relationships that stand the test of time.

How a Lack of Self-Awareness in Relationships Can Destroy the Relationship

It is important to grasp how the absence of self-awareness can sneak in and harm the bond you hold dear. Here are five everyday scenarios that show just how this can unfold:

1. Rollercoaster emotions: Imagine dealing with a day full of stress, and that tension spills into your evening with your partner, turning a simple chat into a heated argument. Without self-awareness, it is like stumbling through a dark room, unaware of what is around you. Recognizing your emotional state and managing it could have prevented unnecessary conflicts.

2. Needs lost in translation: Every relationship has unique needs—be it quality time, words of encouragement, a comforting touch, helpful actions, or thoughtful gifts. A lack of self-awareness might lead to the intentional neglect of these needs. For instance, someone might crave quality time but end up buried in work, oblivious to their emotional needs. This self-induced neglect can sow dissatisfaction and friction in the relationship.

3. Reality distorted by baggage: Without self-awareness, our perception of truth may be distorted by past experiences, biases, or defense mechanisms. For example, someone who has experienced heartbreak may interpret harmless actions as signs of betrayal. Self-awareness helps clear this fog, preventing unnecessary suspicion and tension.

4. Muffled communication: Effective communication is the cornerstone of a relationship, while self-awareness is the secret ingredient for its success. When individuals lack self-awareness, they may struggle to articulate their feelings, needs, and expectations. For

instance, consider a scenario where a partner feels overwhelmed by household chores but struggles to voice this concern. This lack of clarity and open communication can result in underlying resentment and frequent arguments and ultimately lead to a breakdown in the overall communication within the relationship.

5. Unmarked territories of boundaries: Boundaries play a vital role in fostering respectful and healthy relationships. By being self-aware, individuals can effectively establish and maintain these boundaries, ultimately contributing to the strength of the relationship. Consider a scenario where a partner unknowingly crosses personal boundaries, leading the other person to feel disrespected. This breach of boundaries often results in conflict and dissatisfaction, potentially causing strain in the relationship. Therefore, individuals must communicate and uphold their boundaries to ensure mutual respect and understanding within the relationship.

Now, recognizing these pitfalls is just the beginning. It might seem disheartening, but the good news is that self-awareness is not a fixed destination; it is a journey. It can be nurtured and grown. So, even if the road ahead seems uncertain, there is always room to discover more about yourself and strengthen the foundations of your relationships.

Identifying Triggers

Navigating through the maze of overthinking can be like solving a complex puzzle, especially in the context of relationships. Recognizing triggers and understanding personal patterns that lead to overthinking is crucial in reclaiming peace of mind.

Overthinking often stems from a lack of trust, and understanding the reasons behind it can be enlightening. It might be rooted in past wounds—times when you felt hurt or abandoned, leaving a lingering fear that history might repeat itself. Feelings of insecurity can also fuel overthinking, making you question the sincerity of those around you. Moreover, the desire to control external factors can escalate into a web of overanalyzing, where every move and motive becomes suspect.

Unchecked overthinking has a knack for transforming healthy relationships into toxic ones. When you let those relentless thoughts run amok, they create a distrust between you and the people you hold dear. The internal chatter convinces you of things that are not necessarily true, like the idea that your loved ones do not genuinely care. This distortion can lead to a cascade of challenges, from ineffective communication and guardedness to anxiety and neglect of self-care.

There is hope if you find yourself caught in the web of overthinking and want to break free.

- Start by reconnecting with your partner through open communication. Be honest about your feelings, both with yourself and them. Make it clear that while you may need their support, you are taking accountability for your emotions. Your partner is not responsible for regulating your emotions, but they can be an anchor in your journey.

- If that seems overwhelming, begin by vocalizing your thoughts and feelings privately. Whether through journaling or speaking aloud to yourself, this process helps untangle the mess of emotions and reveals their roots. Recognizing that feelings, while valid, may not always align with logical reasoning is a powerful revelation.

- Self-awareness and self-reflection are your allies in stopping the overthinking cycle. Notice your thoughts, challenge them, reframe them when necessary, and practice acceptance of aspects beyond your control. Mindfulness and meditation can offer a sense of control over your thoughts while journaling and gratitude practices reshape your perspective.

- Setting self-care boundaries is another effective tool. By not allowing unhelpful thoughts to occupy too much mental space, you create room for more objective thinking. Overthinking tends to cause overwhelming feelings, but redirecting your energy toward constructive thoughts can make a significant difference.

These strategies can be powerful when used alongside psychotherapy. While self-help is valuable, therapists provide a unique perspective, helping you explore your past, understand your feelings, and determine the best approaches for your well-being. In a nonjudgmental space, therapy becomes a compass guiding you through the complex terrain of your thoughts and emotions. Remember, seeking help is okay; sometimes, a little guidance can lead to profound breakthroughs.

Understanding Emotions: Gaining a Deeper Understanding of Your Emotional Responses in Relationships

Emotions are our natural responses to what life throws our way. When you get good news, happiness sets in. When you face a threat, fear creeps up. It is as straightforward as that.

These emotional reactions are not just passive experiences. They are like silent decision-makers influencing our daily choices. Ever notice how you decide what to do based on whether you feel upbeat, ticked off, down, bored, or annoyed? Emotions have a say in that.

The activities we choose to do in our free time are often related to the emotions they evoke. For instance, you might decide to spend a quiet evening with a book when you feel relaxed while opting for a brisk workout to shake off a dull day.

Understanding these emotional cues is not about diving into complex psychology. It is about having a grip on your own internal compass. When you can name what you are feeling and why, it is like having a more precise map through the daily chaos. It is not about overthinking; it is about steering with more awareness.

Understanding Your Emotions

Navigating the intricate landscape of emotions is not just a psychological exercise but crucial for your overall well-being. Your emotions are like messengers from your body, offering insights into what is happening inside. For instance, a sense of letdown might bring a mix of anger, fear, and sadness—your body's way of communicating a response.

Sure, not all emotions are easy to deal with; shame, in particular, can be downright uncomfortable. However, the key is not in avoiding these feelings but in how you react to them. Understanding your emotional experience involves recognizing which part of your body responds to a particular emotion. The more connected you are with yourself, the better equipped you become to face life's challenges. It is about comprehending why something hits you a certain way.

If you find yourself stuck in a particular emotion, such as anger, it can negatively impact your well-being in the long run. Evidence suggests that being trapped in anger can negatively impact your physical health. However, being aware of and approaching your feelings with love and kindness can help ease anger. Often, anger masks deeper emotions like hurt and sadness, making it crucial to acknowledge all emotions as they come.

Beyond personal well-being, emotional awareness spills into your relationships. Much of how we respond to our partners is influenced by our histories. Knowing your trigger points and emotional responses is vital.

Understanding yourself allows you to communicate your needs, navigate sore spots, and contribute positively to your relationships. Suppose you struggle to connect with your emotions. In that case, it may hinder difficult conversations in your relationship or lead you to believe the grass is greener elsewhere. However, this may be a recurring pattern, and fear of emotional responses can result in a string of unsuccessful relationships.

Moreover, parenting, with its daily challenges, puts your emotional responses to the test. Coming home to chaos after a demanding day might trigger a reaction. It is crucial to understand what exactly you are reacting to—is it the frustrations at work, the feeling of being unheard, or something else lingering from the day? Recognizing your own journey, understanding life's impact on you, and identifying your triggers can transform you into a more patient and responsive parent. After all, your role is not just to manage your emotions but to guide your little ones in navigating and naming theirs. So, in life's journey, let your emotions be your allies, guiding you toward self-awareness, healthier relationships, and more effective parenting.

The Key Elements of Emotions

When we look at the intricacies of emotions, it becomes apparent that it is widely agreed that these complex states comprise three integral components: subjective experiences, physiological responses, and behavioral reactions. Let's break down each part to get a clearer picture.

- Subjective experiences: At the heart of every emotion lies the subjective experience, often referred to as a stimulus. It is the starting point, the trigger that sets the emotional ball rolling. Here's the catch: While basic emotions are universal and experienced by all, the subjective experiences that give rise to them are intensely personal. It can be as mundane as seeing a color or as profound as losing a loved one or tying the knot. The intensity of these experiences can evoke a spectrum of emotions; interestingly, these emotions can vary widely from person to person. For instance, the loss of a loved one might evoke anger and regret in one individual while another experiences profound sadness.

- Physiological responses: Have you ever felt your heart race with fear? That is your body's autonomic nervous system responding to the emotion you are going through. This system regulates involuntary bodily responses and is linked to fight-or-flight instincts. Many psychologists propose that our physiological responses to emotions played a crucial role in our evolution and survival as humans throughout history. Studies suggest that our physiological responses are most robust when our facial expressions closely align with the emotion we are experiencing. Simply put, our facial expressions resemble a physical echo of our emotions.

- Behavioral responses: Now, let's talk about the visible aspect—the behavioral response. This is the outward expression of the emotion bubbling within. Smiles, grimaces, laughs, and sighs are all part of the behavioral responses. However, it is not a one-size-fits-all scenario. While many facial expressions are considered universal (like a frown indicating sadness), societal norms and individual upbringings weave into our behavioral responses. Love, for example, is expressed differently from person to person and across various cultures, highlighting the role of societal and personal influences in shaping how emotions manifest in our actions.

So, emotions are a multi-layered symphony, where your personal experiences, physiological reactions, and outward expressions all play unique roles in creating the intricate tapestry of human emotional experience.

Emotional Suppression

Emotional suppression is like sweeping uncomfortable thoughts and feelings under the mental rug. Whether through distraction, numbing with substances, overeating, or intense physical activity, people find various ways to divert attention from internal turmoil. This coping mechanism often leads to rumination, a ceaseless cycle of overthinking and analyzing suppressed emotions, amplifying stress and anxiety. Repressed emotions stemming from unprocessed traumatic experiences linger in the subconscious.

While emotional suppression is sometimes necessary for social cohesion or professional demands, chronic suppression can lead to anxiety and depression, especially in cases of narcissistic abuse or unresolved trauma. Societal expectations often force individuals to bottle up emotions, maintaining a façade in public spaces (Elsig, 2022). The inability to express emotions authentically can result in a mental tug-of-war, leaving individuals grappling with unaddressed feelings that persist beneath the surface.

Managing Your Emotions

Recognizing and managing emotional triggers is like mastering the art of navigating a labyrinth—you have to tread carefully but with purpose. Here is a guide for you:

Identifying Triggers

1. Acknowledge physical signals: Heart pounding, stomach in knots, shaky limbs, sweaty palms—these are your body's subtle cries for attention. When these signals light up, hit pause. Acknowledge them; they are the breadcrumbs leading to your emotional trigger.

2. Trace back feelings: Reflect on what just occurred to spark these emotions. It is like detective work, linking the current situation to past triggers. If the connection is not crystal clear, embrace the mystery. Dive deeper into your emotions with genuine curiosity.

3. Pattern recognition: Observe any recurring themes. Are there common threads in your triggers? Recognizing patterns provides clarity for future encounters.

Managing As They Come

Once you have uncovered those emotional triggers, the temptation might be to sidestep the situations causing them. Seems straightforward, right? However, life does not come with a manual for evading every challenging moment. Unpleasant emotions are part of the package, dropping in unannounced from time to time.

So, rather than sketching out a grand escape plan, it is about gearing up to confront those triggers in your everyday routine. It is not about dodging the storms but learning to navigate the unpredictable weather of life.

1. Acceptance of emotions: Understand it is okay to feel whatever you feel. Sadness, anger, fear—they are all part of being human. Remind yourself gently of the present, offering compassion rather than judgment.

2. Strategic retreats: Do not hesitate to step back if the emotional storm becomes overwhelming. It is not about weakness but a tactical move to regain composure. Give yourself a moment to breathe, physically and emotionally.

3. Open communication: Most people do not intentionally try to push your emotional buttons. Their actions might be a result of

their own triggers. Opening up about your feelings can promote understanding and prevent similar situations in the future.

In this self-help journey, compassion is your compass. The key is not avoidance but understanding and navigating the maze of emotions. You are not alone; we are all figuring this out. It is about embracing authenticity and finding strength in vulnerability. Let's navigate this labyrinth with wisdom and heart.

How to Increase Self-Awareness With Your Partner

Building self-awareness within a relationship is a journey that involves both personal reflection and shared experiences. Here are practical steps to enhance self-awareness with your partner:

1. Incorporating mindfulness practices like meditation into your daily routine can help you tune into your thoughts and emotions, fostering a deeper understanding of yourself.

2. By setting aside time for meditation, you can create a peaceful and focused state of mind, allowing you to observe your thoughts without judgment and develop a greater awareness of your inner self. This enhanced self-awareness can improve emotional regulation and reduce stress and overall well-being.

3. Regularly engaging in self-inquiry involves asking yourself questions about your feelings, reactions, and desires. By engaging in this introspective dialogue, you can promote self-discovery and gain a deeper understanding of yourself.

4. Keeping a journal to document your thoughts and emotions is a valuable practice for self-reflection and self-awareness. Writing can serve as a therapeutic outlet, allowing you to express your feelings

and gain insights into your inner world. It also lets you track patterns and changes in your emotions and thought processes, providing valuable information for personal growth and development.

5. Read more fiction to boost empathy. Immerse yourself in characters' experiences to broaden your perspective and emotional intelligence.

6. Carve out dedicated time for self-reflection to create physical and mental space and allow the independent processing of thoughts and feelings.

7. Practice active listening. Listening to your partner's words and emotions enhances your understanding of yourself and your relationship dynamics.

8. Actively challenge your perspectives and assumptions. Be open to alternative viewpoints, fostering a more flexible and nuanced self-awareness.

9. It's important to seek feedback from your partner, as it can provide valuable insights into how your behaviors impact each other and highlight areas for personal growth.

10. Honest communication allows you to understand each other's perspectives and can lead to a deeper understanding of your relationship dynamics. This feedback can help you work towards positive changes and improvements in your relationship.

11. Understanding and defining your core values and positive traits is essential to developing a strong sense of self-awareness. Take the time to reflect on what truly matters to you and recognize your unique strengths and qualities. This self-reflection will help you better understand yourself and guide you in making decisions that align with your values and strengths.

12. Consider seeking out the expertise of a relationship coach. These professionals can provide personalized strategies, tools, and insights tailored to your specific needs, helping you to gain a deeper understanding of yourself and improve the dynamics within your relationships.

By integrating these practices, you not only foster self-awareness but also contribute to a more connected and understanding partnership.

Exercise

1. Find a quiet and comfortable space where you can reflect without distractions.
2. Have a pen and paper or a digital device ready to jot down your thoughts.
3. Take a few deep breaths to center yourself before starting.

Reflection questions:

1. Greatest talents or skills:
   a. Which talent or skill gives you the greatest sense of pride or satisfaction?
   b. What talents or skills do you admire most in others?
   c. What talent or skill do you wish to develop for yourself?
2. Personality traits:
   a. List your five most outstanding characteristics.
   b. Identify your two most significant weaknesses.

3. Values and importance:

    a. Name ten things that are important to you.

4. Public vs. private you:

    a. How is the public you different from the private you?

    b. What makes it hard to be yourself around others?

5. Perceptions:

    a. What do you least want people to think about you?

6. Authenticity:

    a. Identify the people, places, and activities that allow you to be fully yourself.

7. Proud moments:

    a. Name three things you are most proud of.

8. Life goals:

    a. What do you hope to achieve in life?

9. Defining yourself:

    a. Name three things that you are.

    b. Name three things that you are not.

10. Representation:

    a. Choose something that represents you (e.g., a song, animal, flower, symbol) and explain why.

11. Self-perception:

    a. What do you like most about yourself?

    b. What do you like least about yourself?

12. Role models:

    a. Name two people you admire and explain why.

13. Joy and impact:

    a. List five things you love to do.

    b. Identify things that make you happy and why.

14. Impact on Others:

    a. How do you want to impact the lives of others?

Take the time to reflect deeply on these questions. Consider revisiting this exercise periodically to track your personal growth and understanding of yourself.

After delving into a deeper understanding of yourself, the upcoming chapter will empower you to recognize and address your negative thought patterns readily. This heightened self-awareness will serve as a foundation for your journey toward positive change and personal growth.

3.
Rewiring Negative Thoughts to End Self-Sabotage

*Your thoughts carry you wherever you want to go.
Weak thoughts do not have the energy to carry you far!*

–ISRAELMORE AYIVOR

What Are Cognitive Distortions?

Cognitive distortions are like subtle habits in our thinking, often veering toward the negative when we are dealing with feelings of depression or anxiety. Imagine them as little glitches in our thought process, casting a shadow that makes things appear gloomier than they really are.

Our brains create mental shortcuts to make thinking more efficient—like opting for the express lane instead of navigating the full complexity of every thought (Pollock, 2023). These shortcuts can oversimplify, turning intricate ideas into all-or-nothing scenarios, posing a challenge.

These distortions have a knack for making us perceive the glass as perpetually half-empty. Over time, they can become companions to mental health conditions, settling in comfortably alongside depression.

But here is the uplifting part—these distortions are not permanent fixtures. We can show them the door with a bit of mental spring cleaning. By recognizing and addressing these thinking hiccups, we essentially tell our brain, "Let's take a detour from this negative path, shall we?"

The journey of self-awareness and learning involves identifying cognitive distortions, which is like shedding light on the shadowy corners of our minds. Once we recognize these distortions, we can begin to reframe our thoughts, transforming shades of gray into a vibrant spectrum of understanding.

Causes and Triggers

Cognitive distortions are not born overnight; they simmer and develop over time like a complex recipe for mental confusion. Researchers believe that stress, negative life events, and even the subtle, continuous drip of smaller negative experiences, like less-than encouraging words from parents or caregivers, contribute to the genesis of these thinking patterns (Huziej, 2023).

Picture it as a puzzle with various pieces—our thoughts, behaviors, and emotions intricately woven together. There is no single culprit, but rather a mix of factors that create the tapestry of cognitive distortions. Think of it as a process: Stress and negative life events play a leading role, creating the conditions for distorted thoughts to show up later in life.

Cognitive distortions often accompany mental health conditions such as depression and anxiety. While they are more likely to be present in individuals facing these challenges, it is unclear whether they are the cause or the consequence. Evidence suggests that they are more like companions in the journey rather than one causing the other.

Imagine a trigger as the spark that ignites the cognitive distortion fire. A typical trigger is the downward depression spiral, which is a series of negative thoughts, feelings, and behaviors that keep turning back on themselves, resulting in a never-ending cycle of pessimism. It is like being stuck in a vortex, with one lousy thought feeding into the next, making the situation increasingly difficult.

How Cognitive Distortions Impact Your Well-Being

Cognitive distortions can have a significant influence on our well-being, causing unpleasant feelings such as anxiety, depression, and other mental health disorders. They affect our experience of the world, frequently leading us to see things in disproportionately negative terms, such as an explicit line between the good and the bad.

1. Labeling ourselves: Cognitive distortions can lead us to categorize ourselves or others inaccurately. For example, you may unfairly identify yourself as a "failure" or as "stupid" or call your partner a "jerk." These false labels can become extremely destructive, instilling self-hatred and causing interpersonal difficulties.

2. Questioning our thoughts: Cognitive distortion can also erode our confidence in our own thoughts and feelings. For example, if you start to feel capable and successful in your job, distorted thinking may lead you to doubt those feelings, triggering anxiety and persistent worry.

3. Presuming negative thoughts: Cognitive distortion also leads us to believe that our emotions consistently represent reality. For example, suppose you feel inadequate at work. In that case, you may start to believe it is an absolute reality. This can result in a chain reaction of negative ideas and feelings, creating a cycle of self-doubt and pessimism.

Cognitive distortions can act as a fog, clouding our perception of reality and influencing our emotions in unhelpful ways. Understanding and correcting these distortions is vital for establishing a better and more balanced psychological state.

How Cognitive Distortions Result in Self-Sabotage in Relationships

Have you ever caught yourself getting lost in negative thoughts about a person or situation? Even worse, have those automatic negative thoughts ever led you to make regrettable choices? These tricky mental maneuvers are what we call cognitive distortions, and the fallout often translates to self-sabotage.

It's normal to view situations through the filter of cognitive distortions. However, these distortions can evoke negative emotions, encourage unhelpful behaviors, and disrupt intimacy. A relationship resembles a delicate dance, requiring effort, understanding, communication, trust, and loyalty. Each person's thinking and behavioral patterns can significantly impact the relationship's health (Das, 2023).

Cognitive distortions function as subconscious filters or biases, shaping how we see connections and guiding our behaviors and judgments. This may aggravate worry and tension. Our brains continually absorb large amounts of information, so cognitive distortions influence our viewpoints. As a result, they can cause ripple effects in our interactions with others around us, influencing the dynamics of our most meaningful relationships.

We all engage in an internal dialogue and occasionally misread our partners. However, when cognitive distortions enter the scene, they can set the stage for conflict in your relationship. It is like adding a layer of static to your communication channels, making navigating the complexities of emotional connection more challenging. Recognizing and addressing these distortions can be a game-changer, helping to untangle the knots and foster a healthier, more harmonious relationship.

Causes of Self-Sabotaging in Relationships

Causes of self-sabotage in relationships can often be rooted in various factors that shape our perceptions and behaviors. Let's break down some common triggers in a straightforward and relatable manner:

1. Childhood trauma: Childhood experiences, especially if marked by trauma like a parent leaving, can create an overgeneralization of cognitive distortion. For instance, if someone's mother left when they were a child, they might fear that everyone, including their current partner, will also leave them. This fear can lead to overthinking, like interpreting a late arrival as a sign of impending abandonment.

2. Fear of getting hurt or abandoned: This fear is closely tied to overgeneralization, similar to the scenario mentioned above. A past experience of being hurt or abandoned can make someone overly cautious and prone to overthinking their partner's actions, such as scrutinizing late-night returns.

3. Trust issues from past negative experiences: Trust issues often stem from past betrayals, triggering overgeneralization and jumping to conclusions. For instance, if someone experienced betrayal in a previous relationship, they might generalize that all men are cheaters. This can lead to overthinking, like obsessing over their partner's innocent conversations on social media.

4. Excessively high or unrealistic expectations: Unrealistic expectations, often driven by childhood experiences or insecurities, can create a constant need for validation. For instance, if someone grew up with high academic expectations, they might project this perfectionism onto their partner, expecting expensive gifts as proof of love. This can result in overthinking and overanalyzing every aspect of the relationship.

5. Poor self-esteem: Low self-esteem often stems from a tendency to think in absolutes and impose strict "should/must" beliefs on oneself. This can create a sense of inadequacy and lead to feelings of not being good enough. For example, a work failure might cause someone to believe they are an overall failure, impacting their self-worth in the relationship. This self-doubt can fuel overthinking and a persistent sense of not being good enough.

6. Lack of relationship skills: A deficiency in relationship skills, influenced by various cognitive distortions, can contribute to self-sabotage. Negative thinking patterns, encompassing all of the cognitive distortions listed below, can lead to overthinking and hinder the ability to build positive relationships. Addressing these thinking patterns becomes crucial to breaking the cycle of self-sabotage in relationships.

Nine Cognitive Distortions That Can Lead to Overthinking and Self-Sabotage in Your Relationships

Understanding cognitive distortions is like uncovering the peculiarities of our brain—it is not a flaw or disorder but a natural outcome of how our minds function.

Our brains tend to simplify things for efficiency, often choosing the fastest solution when processing information or solving problems. This instinctual shortcutting is a survival mechanism rooted in our ancient past. Picture this: You spot a rod on the road, and without a second thought, your brain shouts, "Snake!" It is a split-second prioritization of your safety, a trick from when our ancestors navigated a different, more perilous world (Karadeniz, 2018).

We are now far from the woods our ancestors roamed. Cognitive distortions are not necessarily a problem, but they can lead to psychological symptoms and negative thoughts. Let's look at nine cognitive distortions that could cause overthinking and self-sabotage.

1. All-or-nothing thinking: Seeing things in absolute terms—either entirely successful or a total failure—is a distortion. Recognizing life's nuances is vital to overcoming this mindset.

2. Overgeneralization: Making sweeping statements based on a single event. Acknowledging that one experience does not define all people helps break free from overgeneralization.

3. Mental filtering: Focusing solely on the negatives and disregarding any positives in a situation can lead to distorted thinking. Practicing mindfulness and identifying positive aspects are helpful tools to combat this cognitive distortion.

4. Magnification: Drawing conclusions without sufficient evidence or blowing the importance of negatives out of proportion. Developing critical thinking skills and staying present are crucial to overcoming magnification.

5. Emotional reasoning: Assuming feelings reflect reality. Differentiating between emotions and thoughts, relying on facts and logical reasoning, helps counter this distortion.

6. "Should" statements: Setting unrealistic standards for ourselves and then criticizing or punishing ourselves when we fail to meet them can damage our well-being. Instead, showing compassion, being realistic about our capabilities, and treating ourselves with kindness can help counteract this harmful behavior.

7. Labeling and mislabeling: Assigning global labels based on a single behavior, leading to biases and stereotypes. Avoiding assumptions and appreciating the complexity of individuals helps combat this distortion.

8. Personalization: Some people believe they are solely responsible for every problem, unexpected situation, or mistake. Recognizing shared responsibility can alleviate this distortion.

9. Jumping to conclusions: Engaging in behaviors such as assuming knowledge about others' feelings or actions (mind-reading) and predicting future events (fortune-telling) is not permitted. Challenging these assumptions and focusing on what is observable in the present is essential to combat jumping to conclusions.

These cognitive distortions, while natural, can impact our thoughts and behaviors. Recognizing them is the first step toward fostering healthier thinking patterns and avoiding self-sabotage in our relationships and everyday lives.

How to Stop Self-Sabotaging in Relationships

Ending self-sabotaging in relationships requires self-awareness and a commitment to positive change. Here is how you can break free from destructive patterns and cultivate healthier connections:

1. Own up to your actions: Taking responsibility for your behavior is the first step in halting self-sabotage. Recognize the role you have played in past relationship challenges. Once you confront these behaviors, you can actively work on changing them.

2. Spot your triggers: Uncover the triggers that set off your self-sabotaging tendencies. Is it a partner expressing a need for commitment, or perhaps certain places that make you uneasy? Identifying these triggers empowers you to find healthier ways to navigate and cope with your emotions.

3. Open up and share: Despite the fear of intimacy or abandonment, expressing your feelings to your partner is crucial. Sharing your struggles helps your partner understand your experience, fostering a collaborative approach to working through issues together.

4. Challenge distorted thoughts: Confront and overcome cognitive distortions by questioning negative thought patterns. Are you seeing situations in black-and-white terms? Challenge these distortions to foster a more balanced and realistic perspective.

5. Prioritize personal well-being: Boost your overall well-being, vital in cultivating healthier relationships. Take care of yourself physically, mentally, and emotionally, ensuring you bring the best version of yourself into the partnership.

6. Seek professional guidance: Recognize that it can be challenging to stop self-sabotage. Seeking professional support, such as seeing

a therapist, can provide valuable insights into recognizing harmful habits and recovering from past traumatic experiences. Under their guidance, you can break free from repetitive cycles of unhealthy relationships and develop essential coping skills. Remember, asking for help is a courageous first step toward meaningful transformation.

Recognizing and addressing self-sabotaging behaviors is not always easy. However, it is an essential journey toward healthier, more fulfilling relationships. These steps pave the way for positive change and create the space for meaningful connections to thrive.

How Do You Identify and Manage Cognitive Distortions?

A little self-reflection and close observation of your thought processes are necessary to determine whether you are entangled in the web of cognitive distortions. Here are some practical ways to help you determine whether cognitive distortions are at work:

1. Check-in with yourself: Regularly assess your mental landscape. Take moments throughout the day to reflect on your thoughts and feelings. Are there recurring patterns or themes that stand out? Being mindful of your mental state is the first step.

2. Document your thoughts: Keep a mental diary by jotting down your predominant thoughts. Note when these thoughts occur, whether they are linked to a specific place or situation. Recognizing patterns in your thinking can shed light on potential cognitive distortions.

3. Connect thoughts to emotions: Once you have identified a thought, pinpoint the emotion it triggers. Understanding the emotional impact of your thoughts adds depth to your self-awareness. It can highlight areas where cognitive distortions may be influencing your feelings.

4. Group thoughts by theme: During a specified time frame, take the time to organize your recorded thoughts by identifying common themes. This deliberate process will enable you to recognize overarching patterns and provide valuable insight into the specific areas of your life where cognitive distortions may be more prevalent.

5. Change roles: Step into a different perspective. Consider how someone else might view the situation if your thoughts are predominantly negative. This shift can offer a more balanced outlook and help you break free from distorted thinking.

6. Examine the evidence: Evaluate the evidence supporting your thoughts. Are they grounded in reality, or are they based on assumptions? Scrutinizing the facts can reveal whether your thinking aligns with the actual circumstances.

7. The sum of its parts: Break down complex situations into smaller components. This helps avoid the all-or-nothing thinking that often accompanies cognitive distortions. By examining individual elements, you gain a more nuanced understanding.

8. Avoid generalization: Resist the urge to generalize based on isolated incidents. Recognize that one negative event does not define an entire situation or person. Avoiding sweeping generalizations contributes to more balanced thinking.

9. Skip speculation: Steer clear of speculative thoughts about future events or others' intentions. Stick to what you know and have evidence for rather than diving into unfounded assumptions.

10. Replace "shoulds": Switching from using rigid "shoulds" to more flexible language can be beneficial. Instead of imposing strict expectations, it is helpful to acknowledge alternatives and consider a range

of possibilities. This approach fosters a more realistic and adaptable mindset, allowing for greater flexibility and open-mindedness.

11. Do cost-benefit analysis: Consider both the advantages and disadvantages of your ideas and decisions. This practical approach helps you make more logical decisions by assisting you in evaluating different possibilities

By incorporating these techniques into your self-reflection routine, you can gain insight into your mental processes and recognize if cognitive distortions affect your thinking.

Exercise
Part 1: Identify Your Cognitive Distortions

1. Unrealistic expectations: Example: Expecting your partner to fulfill all your emotional needs without communication.

2. Personalization: Example: Blaming yourself for every disagreement or problem in the relationship.

3. Magnifying: Example: Exaggerating the significance of a minor flaw or mistake made by your partner.

4. Disqualifying the positive: Example: Brushing off compliments or positive gestures from your partner as insignificant.

Part 2: Reflection on Your Distortions

1. Identify your distorted thoughts: Reflect on your relationship and identify specific instances where you might be prone to these cognitive distortions.

2. Examine the patterns: Describe the thoughts, feelings, and behaviors that accompany each distortion. For example, if you have unrealistic expectations, you might feel disappointed and behave passively-aggressively.

3. Impact: Explore how these distortions affect your relationship dynamics. Consider if they contribute to misunderstandings, conflicts, or emotional distance.

Part 3: Questioning Your Thoughts

1. Validity: Ask yourself if these distorted thoughts are objectively true or if cognitive distortions influence them.

2. Evidence: List evidence supporting your distorted thoughts and evidence against them. This helps you objectively evaluate the validity of your perceptions.

3. Alternative thoughts: Generate alternative thoughts that counteract the negative distortions. For instance, if you magnify a small mistake, consider a more balanced perspective, acknowledging your partner's overall positive qualities.

Reflecting on your cognitive distortions is a crucial step in fostering healthier relationships. This worksheet serves as a tool to bring awareness to your thought patterns, understand their impact, and develop alternative, more balanced perspectives. Keep in mind that the goal of this process is to develop and progress both your relationship and yourself.

As we delve into the intricacies of managing negative thought patterns, it becomes evident that self-care plays a pivotal role. Nurturing yourself is not just a means of personal well-being but a powerful tool to empower you to overcome internal struggles and navigate your relationships more effectively. In the next chapter, we will explore the transformative impact of self-care on your inner resilience and its profound influence on the dynamics of your connections with others.

Engaging in Self-Care Practices and Improving Relationship Quality

4.
The Path to a Calm and Anxiety-Free Relationship

Most people do not understand why love makes us vulnerable or open.
It is because love, to be fully expressed and through your being, begins to
eliminate all the fears, all the insecurities, and all the anxieties that are
inconsistent with itself.

—Betty Bethards

How Stress and Anxiety Can Lead to Overthinking and Vice Versa

Constantly replaying thoughts in our minds, known as overthinking, is closely associated with stress and anxiety. These psychological states interact with each other in a complex way. Stress and worry are common conditions for overthinking to thrive, but it is not limited to that; overthinking is also connected to our self-perception and uncertainties.

Stress is a normal reaction to difficult circumstances. However, it can become a chronic burden if we do not know how to manage it. Stress causes our minds to become overly analytical and susceptible to intrusive thoughts. It is like a never-ending cycle: Stress leads to a rush of thoughts, leading to overanalyzing.

Anxiety and stress often go hand in hand. Anxiety involves excessive worry and fear, causing us to constantly dwell on past events or obsess over potential future outcomes. This ongoing mental activity leads to overthinking as our minds grapple with various possibilities, consequences, and imagined threats.

Research tells us there is a two-way street between overthinking and stress. It is a bit like the classic "chicken-and-egg" puzzle—high levels of stress, anxiety, and even depression can feed into overthinking, while overthinking can make stress-related conditions worse. It becomes a cycle, intensifying both overthinking and the mental health challenges that come with it (Witman, 2023).

Another factor that contributes to overthinking is the combination of self-esteem and self-doubt. When we question our value or constantly second-guess our decisions, we fuel the fire of overthinking. This creates a double burden—external stressors and internal struggles keep us in a perpetual state of overthinking.

It is important to recognize and understand this complex relationship between stress, anxiety, and overthinking. However, there are ways to break free from this cycle. Have you ever tried practicing mindfulness or simple stress management techniques? They can truly make a significant difference. Additionally, cognitive behavioral therapy is also a valuable option to consider.

We are constantly trying to navigate our minds' intricate and complex pathways, which can be challenging. However, it is not impossible. By identifying and addressing the underlying causes of our inner turmoil and discovering healthier coping mechanisms, we can gradually quiet the chaos in our minds and attain a sense of tranquility. It is essential to take each step of this journey patiently and deliberately—you have the strength to overcome this.

What Is Relationship Anxiety?

Relationship anxiety can bring about times of doubt, constant worry, and a never-ending need for validation in a relationship. It feels like a fog of uncertainty and a constant need for reassurance over the potential for a great relationship. This type of anxiousness might indicate an insecure attachment style and frequently stems from early childhood attachments.

Imagine finding yourself at the beginning of what appears to be a promising and fulfilling relationship. Two-way communication flows effortlessly, and everything seems aligned for a blissful future. Amidst the excitement, there is an underlying uncertainty and persistent questions that cannot be ignored.

"What qualities do they truly admire in me?" Will the initial spark eventually dim? "How long until challenges arise?" These doubts can linger, even after the exchange of heartfelt "I love yous."

If you have ever found yourself caught up in these thoughts, you might be familiar with relationship anxiety. It is like an unwanted companion that tags along, making you second-guess the connection you have found.

When dread begins to seep in and throws a shadow on the possibility of a deep and meaningful connection, it is a reasonable concern. After all, relationships play a significant role in our lives. However, occasionally, this anxiety gets so bad that it prevents the relationship from developing or even from starting in the first place.

You are not alone if you have been struggling with these concerns. Understanding that relationship anxiety is common is the first step toward finding ways to navigate and manage it, leading to a more fulfilling and healthy connection.

Roots of Relationship Anxiety

Relationship anxiety often originates from a combination of past experiences and personal characteristics. These factors contribute to a range of causes that can lead to feelings of anxiety within relationships. Some common causes that can contribute to relationship anxiety include:

- Attachment styles from childhood: How we bond with our parents or caregivers during childhood has a significant impact. A secure attachment style develops when parents consistently show love and affection. However, suppose a child constantly seeks reassurance and depends on their caregivers. In that case, these behaviors may continue into adulthood and affect romantic relationships. People with anxious attachment styles may doubt their value, be alert for signs of decreasing interest from their partners, and fear the prospect of losing them.

- Impact of past experiences: When someone has experienced doubt about their worth or attractiveness in a past relationship, it can lead to anxiety in new relationships. Just as being stung by a bee can make you cautious of any buzzing sound, past experiences can make a person constantly question the stability and authenticity of their current relationship.

- Self-perception and esteem: Low self-worth can negatively impact various aspects of life, including relationships. Individuals with poor self-esteem may constantly question their partner's feelings and worry whether they genuinely deserve love. This self-doubt can jeopardize the stability of the relationship by leading to suspicions of infidelity and other issues.

- Communication dynamics: When partners struggle to share their feelings or discuss the relationship's direction openly, it creates a crack in the foundation of communication. This gap can lead to anxiety and uncertainty, breeding doubts about affection and casting shadows over the relationship's future.

Understanding these causes is essential in addressing relationship anxiety. It is a journey that involves recognizing patterns, fostering open communication, and, when needed, seeking support to build a more secure and fulfilling connection.

Indicators of Relationship Anxiety

It is crucial to recognize symptoms of relationship anxiety to foster a happy and healthy relationship. The following are common indicators that you might be experiencing relationship anxiety:

Doubting your partner's feelings: Questioning the authenticity of your partner's emotions and the genuineness of their feelings for you.

- Constantly seeking reassurance: Continuously seeking validation and support from your partner in order to alleviate persistent uncertainties and insecurities in the relationship.

- People-pleasing: Striving to constantly fulfill your significant other's needs and desires, even if it comes at the expense of your own physical, emotional, or mental well-being.

- Controlling behavior: Acting in a controlling manner involves monitoring and regulating your partner's movements or interactions, often stemming from fear or insecurity.

- This behavior can manifest in various ways, such as checking their texts, monitoring their social media activity, or questioning their whereabouts. It can also involve attempting to control who they spend time with or what they wear. These actions can indicate underlying trust issues and a need for power and control in the relationship.

- Excessive clinginess: Feeling an ongoing desire to always be in the presence of your partner, displaying clingy behavior in most situations, and finding it challenging to assert independence or self-sufficiency.

- Doubts about compatibility: Holding persistent doubts about the compatibility of your relationship and questioning whether you are truly right for each other.

- Overanalyzing: Reading too much into simple words and actions, searching for hidden meanings and signs of trouble.

- Fear of relationship ending: Constantly feeling like your partner intends to call off the relationship despite no clear evidence supporting this belief.

- Excessive worrying: Spending more time worrying about the relationship than enjoying the positive aspects creates an imbalance in your emotional focus.

- Sabotaging behaviors: Deliberately damaging the relationship, exaggerating minor issues, or testing your partner's loyalty.
- Guarded and aloof behavior: Purposely distancing oneself from a partner in an attempt to avoid potential emotional pain and challenges.

Recognizing these signs enables you to talk openly and reflectively with your partner. Navigating and managing relationship anxiety and seeking support through introspection or expert advice can promote a stronger and more stable bond.

Impact of Relationship Anxiety

Evaluating your behavior in a relationship is essential, but not every sign of concern indicates relationship anxiety. Reflecting on what is going well, changes in communication, and shared emotions is a positive practice. However, if constantly monitoring your partner becomes an exhausting obsession, it may indicate a deeper issue.

Constantly worrying about your relationship can significantly affect the quality of love and intimacy you experience. This persistent anxiety may even lead to the feared outcome of the relationship ending. If you frequently experience relationship anxiety, it can have a negative impact on your well-being and the future of your partnership.

Recognizing these impacts is the first step toward positive change. Persistent anxiety can strain the emotional connection and diminish the overall quality of the relationship. It creates a cycle where fear and doubt overshadow moments of joy and connection, ultimately straining the bond between partners and contributing to instability.

However, it is important to realize that you can take steps to improve your relationship's health and well-being. Seeking help can provide valuable insights and anxiety management techniques through expert advice or open conversations with your partner. You can achieve a more satisfying and enduring relationship by cultivating a more stable emotional connection and learning healthy coping strategies.

Remember, understanding and resolving relationship anxiety is an ongoing process, and taking proactive actions can lead to a healthier and happier relationship.

Overcoming Relationship Anxiety

Navigating relationship anxiety can be a complex journey. However, there are practical strategies to cope with and overcome these challenging feelings. Consider the following steps:

- Open communication: Initiate honest conversations with your partner about worries, expectations, and future aspirations. Sharing doubts and addressing challenges openly is more constructive than dwelling on worst-case scenarios. Clear communication fosters a deeper understanding of the relationship, minimizing uncertainties that may contribute to anxiety.

- Embrace the present: Redirect your focus from future uncertainties to the current moment. Speculating about the longevity of your relationship or potential desirability in the future detracts from appreciating the joy in the present. Managing anxiety involves embracing the present reality and savoring the joy of being with someone you have chosen, who has also chosen you.

- Confront and understand anxiety: Confronting anxiety may seem counterintuitive, but it is a powerful method for regaining emotional control. Investigate the root causes of your anxiety, whether they are tied to past relationships or self-perception issues. Understanding these triggers allows for direct and targeted efforts toward resolution.

- Consider professional therapy: Seeking professional guidance can be valuable in some instances. Therapy offers support in transforming negative thoughts about yourself, addressing self-worth concerns, and refining perceptions of your partner. Therapeutic interventions equip you with practical tools to manage anxiety and prevent potential harm to the relationship.

Remember, overcoming relationship anxiety is a process that may involve a combination of these strategies. Taking proactive steps to address and manage anxiety can contribute to the creation of a more fulfilling and stable relationship.

Signs That Stress Is Affecting Your Relationship

Recognizing when stress starts to seep into your relationship is like noticing the first cracks in a beloved mug—subtle but significant. Here are some signs that stress might be affecting your connection:

- Being the contrarian: Although you typically communicate effectively, lately, it feels like you are speaking different languages to each other. If you find yourself arguing just to be difficult, stress may be influencing your emotions.

- Intimacy hits a speed bump: Remember those lingering kisses and meaningful glances? Lately, it is as if the spark fizzled out. Stress can turn even the most passionate encounters into hurried routines or distant memories.

- Anger unleashed: Your partner accidentally squeezes the toothpaste from the middle again, and suddenly, it is World War III in your bathroom. Stress can turn minor annoyances into raging infernos, leaving both of you scorched and bewildered.

- The paranoia game: You may find yourself creating elaborate theories about your partner's whereabouts or intentions. Stress can cause us to imagine problems where there are none, weakening the trust essential for healthy relationships.

- Every little thing irritates you: Their laugh, their cough, even the way they slurp their soup—it is like nails on a chalkboard. Stress can heighten your sensitivity to the point where every quirk becomes a trigger.

- Craving solitude: You used to be inseparable, but now the thought of spending time together feels suffocating. Stress can make even the warmest embraces feel like straightjackets, driving you to seek solace in solitude.

- General discontent: The laughter that used to fill your home now feels like a distant memory. If you are beginning to feel more like roommates than soulmates, stress may be affecting your relationship.

It is important to view these signs as indicators that it is time to take action rather than as a signal that your relationship is doomed. It is crucial to show compassion and understanding for each other while acknowledging that both of you are dealing with stress. By working together, you can navigate this challenging time and emerge stronger and more connected than before.

How to Deal With Relationship Stress

Navigating through stressful times in a relationship can be challenging, but it is not impossible. Unexpected life events like financial issues or the demands of parenthood can lead to tension and arguments. However, there are loving ways to identify and address the warning signs that stress is affecting your relationship.

- Change of scenery: Ever notice how being cooped up inside can make arguments feel suffocating? Stepping outside and taking a walk together can work wonders. It allows you to breathe in fresh air and gain a new perspective, making difficult conversations feel more manageable.

- Be careful what you say: When emotions are running high, words can carry a lot of force. Use "I" statements to share your feelings rather than laying blame or pointing fingers. Being vulnerable can ease the tension in a fight and make room for understanding.

- Lend a helping hand: Seeking help can seem like accepting defeat when stress is getting to you. Your partner can help with that. Providing assistance, whether taking on household tasks or simply being a listening ear, can have a profound impact. It demonstrates your unity through thick and thin.

- Listen empathically: It is easy to become engrossed in your own beliefs and feelings during a heated disagreement. However, giving your partner your undivided attention for a few minutes makes a big difference. Even if you disagree with them, expressing your interest in what they have to say can ease tension and create a feeling of connection.

- Think of the big picture: Relationship tension often arises from external factors as well as internal issues within yourself and your partner.

These factors can range from family problems to work pressures. By taking the time to identify the root cause of the stress, you can better support each other and work together to overcome obstacles.

- Seek support together: Feeling overwhelmed by stress is expected at times. Seeking help from a couples counselor is not a sign of weakness; it is a brave step toward strengthening relationships. With the support of a qualified expert, you can gain new perspectives, improve communication, and learn strategies to navigate life's challenges.

It is critical to approach each other in stressful situations with kindness, sympathy, and a desire to work through difficult situations together. Recognizing the signs of stress, such as irritability, fatigue, or changes in sleeping patterns, allows you to take proactive steps to manage it effectively. By openly communicating with your loved ones, seeking support, and engaging in stress-relieving activities together, you can weather difficult times, strengthen your bond, and build resilience as a team.

Exercise

Stress in the modern world is like an unwelcome guest who refuses to leave. It infiltrates our lives and causes mental and physical disruption. But there is no need to worry! To help you reduce stress and regain peace of mind, here are some healthy strategies for you to start practicing. (Sherrell, 2022). Breathing exercises calm the mind, relax the body, and make you feel like a Zen master. They are like little pockets of calm in a busy world. Now, let's explore these incredible methods.

Find Your Inner Zen with Alternate Nostril Breathing:

1. Get comfy, whether on the floor or in your favorite chair.
2. Close your eyes and take a few deep breaths to center yourself.

3. Lift your right hand toward your nose.
4. Use your thumb to close your right nostril and inhale deeply through your left.
5. Use your ring finger to close your left nostril and exhale through your right.
6. Keep alternating nostrils to breathe in and out.
7. Repeat this dance for ten rounds, feeling the rhythm of your breath and the calm washing over you.

Do not worry if you feel lightheaded; breathe normally and return to it when you are ready.

Pucker Up for Pursed Lip Breathing:

1. Find your chill spot, whether it is on a chair or the floor.
2. Keep your neck and shoulders loose.
3. Inhale slowly through your nose for two seconds.
4. Purse those lips like you are blowing a kiss and exhale for a count of four.
5. Feel the tension melt away with each breath.
6. Keep whooshing the air out in this way for a few minutes, making those exhales longer each time.

Sink Into Serenity With Resonance Frequency Breathing:

1. Lie down and get cozy with your eyes closed.
2. Take a couple of deep breaths to get in the zone.

3. Inhale for six counts, feeling your belly rise like a balloon.
4. Exhale for six counts, letting that belly deflate like a balloon with a tiny hole.
5. Ride the wave of your breath for up to 10 minutes, soaking in the calm vibes.

Keep It Simple With a Basic Breathing Exercise:

1. Get comfy whether you are standing, sitting, or lying down.
2. Loosen up any tight clothing to let those lungs breathe.
3. Inhale through your nose for a count of five, filling up that belly like a balloon.
4. Exhale through your mouth for another count of five, letting go of all that tension.
5. Repeat this for three to five minutes, feeling lighter with each breath.

Bonus Round: Progressive Muscle Relaxation:

1. Lie down and close your eyes.
2. Take a few deep breaths and let your body sink into the mattress.
3. Tense up one muscle group, like your arms, for a solid ten seconds.
4. Release the tension and let those muscles melt like butter on a hot pancake.
5. Repeat this muscle-tension-release cycle for every muscle group in your body.

Once you have gone through your whole body, reflect on how you feel and enjoy the feeling of peace, calm, and presence.

Incorporating these breathing exercises and muscle relaxation into your daily routine is like giving yourself a big, cozy hug. They are your secret weapons against stress, anxiety, and the general craziness of life.

As we delve deeper into the intricate web of stress and its impact on our lives, one glaring culprit often emerges: perfectionism. We all strive for excellence in our endeavors. However, when the pursuit of perfection becomes an unrelenting demand, it can tip the scales, leaving us drowning in a sea of stress and self-doubt. This is why the next chapter holds the key to breaking free from the shackles of perfectionism. It will explore strategies and techniques that will empower you to embrace imperfection, cultivate self-compassion, and reclaim your peace of mind.

5.
Embracing the Beauty of Imperfection in Relationships

To love another human in all of her splendor and imperfect perfection, it is a magnificent task... tremendous and foolish and human.

–Louise Erdrich

Understanding Perfectionism

Are you among those who find it impossible to resist the need to make everything flawless? Does the idea of anything less than perfect give you the chills? Hold on tight because you could be about to go on a challenging ride that will lead you right into the trap of overthinking.

Imagine that you are faced with a task that needs to be completed. But rather than taking action and finishing the task at hand, you find yourself mired in a never-ending cycle of "buts" and "what ifs." You become immobilized with uncertainty as every possible situation repeats itself in your head like a movie reel.

But why do we torture ourselves like this? What drives us to chase after an ideal that's as elusive as a mirage in the desert? Well, there are a few suspects in this case. Genetics might have a hand in it, programming us with a predisposition for perfection. Then there is upbringing—those childhood lessons about always striving for the best and never settling for anything less. And let's not forget trauma, the silent architect of our need for control in a chaotic world.

Striving for perfection is like trying to grasp water with your bare hands: the tighter you squeeze, the more it slips away. Instead of clarity, you are submerged in a flood of possibilities, overwhelmed by endless "what ifs" that obscure your vision of solid ground. This overwhelming uncertainty leads to paralysis. Stress levels skyrocket, decisions are postponed, and deadlines are missed. You are imprisoned in your own thoughts, unable to break free from the never-ending analysis loop.

Breaking free from the damaging cycle involves recognizing and understanding our perfectionist tendencies and then taking steps to embrace our true selves. Cultivating self-awareness allows us to identify our thought patterns, emotions, and behaviors, leading to a deeper understanding of our motivations and desires. This heightened self-awareness empowers us to make conscious choices and develop a more genuine and fulfilling way of living.

Embracing imperfection involves recognizing that perfection is often unattainable and that settling for "good enough" is sometimes the best choice. It is about releasing ourselves from the relentless pursuit of flawlessness and allowing room for growth, learning, and making mistakes. As we let go of the quest for perfection, we free ourselves from over-analysis and embrace the messy yet beautiful world of existence. In this process, we come to understand that true excellence is not defined by flawlessness but by our willingness to acknowledge and learn from our imperfections.

Causes

Do you ever feel like you are constantly striving for an unattainable level of perfection? No matter how hard you try, your efforts are never quite good enough. There are a few reasons behind this relentless pursuit of perfection.

- Genetics: Studies indicate that perfectionism may occasionally run in families. It is transmitted from one generation to the next as if it were an inherited characteristic. Twin research has even demonstrated that perfectionistic tendencies can be shaped by both heredity and upbringing (Dorwart, 2023).

- Upbringing: Sometimes, you might have parents who set the bar sky-high, constantly pushing you to be the best of the best. Sound familiar? High parental expectations, pressure, and even a hint of control can fuel the perfectionist mindset. You are constantly striving to live up to the impossibly high expectations that were placed on you from the beginning.

- Trauma: Regretfully, many people who battle perfectionism have also experienced some difficult times in their lives. When you look back on your early years, were you ever abused or neglected? Indeed, those encounters remain in your memory. Trauma has the power to permanently alter your perspective of both the outside world and yourself.

Then there are also the cultural and social causes:

- Colleges and universities: You know, those situations where tension can rise as quickly as a pot boiling over on the stove. It is no secret that perfectionism can flourish in academic settings, particularly in professions where the need to do well is ingrained in the curriculum, such as medicine, law, and pharmacy. Being the best of the best is like an unending race that does not allow for anything less than excellence.

- Athletics: Athletes are always in the public eye, and everyone expects them to compete at the highest level. The pressure to be perfect can have a negative impact on athletes and coaches alike. According to research, athletes who strive for perfection or have instructors who push them too much are likelier to burn out and give in to the pressure of their extremely high standards.

- Arts: You know, those areas where originality and critique clash. The pressure to be flawless can be overwhelming for artists, musicians, and dancers. Imagine dedicating your entire being to your work, only to be criticized by others or overshadowed by competitors. Understandably, self-criticism can quickly drain your enthusiasm.

- Social media: Ah, the land of filters, Photoshop, and meticulously managed lifestyles. Images of the "ideal" body and cultural ideals of beauty seem to be thrown at us nonstop. There is this underlying pressure, especially for young women, to live up to those unachievable norms. It is enough to give someone the impression that they are constantly failing.

- Immigration: Many people who come from immigrant families have to bear the burden of their parents' sacrifices. It is expected that you will not only make it through but also beyond all expectations.

For them, it feels like you are fulfilling their aspirations, and anything less than excellence is a betrayal.

Hence, these various elements may have shed light on the factors contributing to your perfectionism. Identifying these underlying influences is a crucial part of understanding the roots of this mindset. Recognizing where it all stems from can be the initial stride toward finding inner peace. Remember that you are not alone in this journey; there is always space for self-compassion along the way.

Types of Perfectionism

Perfectionism is not a one-size-fits-all concept; it comes in various forms, each with its own nuances and challenges. Let's explore these different types to understand better how perfectionism manifests in our lives.

- Self-oriented perfectionism: This is like having an inner critic who will not quit. You set impossibly high standards for yourself and beat yourself up when you do not meet them. It is like you are constantly chasing after this elusive idea of perfection, thinking that your worth is tied to your achievements. And let me tell you, it can be exhausting. On the bright side, self-oriented perfectionists are often driven, hardworking, and super conscientious. Just watch out for that tendency to get lost in a whirlwind of anxiety and worry.

- Other-oriented perfectionism: In this version, you find yourself projecting your perfectionistic tendencies onto someone else—usually a partner, a kid, or even a friend. You are constantly nitpicking at their flaws, pushing them to be the best version of themselves, whether they like it or not. It is like you are trying to mold them into your idea of perfection without considering what they actually want or need. And yeah, it can get pretty controlling. We are all a work in progress, right?

- Socially prescribed perfectionism: This makes you feel like you are living under a microscope and that people are always observing and evaluating your actions. Meeting the expectations of others, be they from your friends, family, or society at large, consumes so much of your time and energy that you lose sight of your true desires. It can be oppressive and feels like you are trapped in an unending game of attempting to live up to some unattainable norm. However, remember that you are more than the culmination of the expectations of others. Due to your unique individuality and imperfections, you are wonderfully human.

Keep in mind that perfectionism is not everything. It is okay to aim for excellence, but not if it compromises your own happiness and well-being. So, go easy on yourself, take a deep breath, and remember that perfection is overrated anyway.

Traits and Symptoms

Perfectionism can show up as a number of qualities and behaviors that frequently go beyond aspiring for perfection. Here are a few typical indicators of excessive perfectionism:

1. Imposing unreachable standards: Perfectionists habitually establish exceedingly high benchmarks and relentlessly pursue excellence. However, their perpetual quest for flawlessness leads to inevitable disappointment, perpetuating a detrimental cycle of self-condemnation and diminished self-esteem.

2. Excessive criticism: Perfectionism correlates with excessive criticism of others and stringent self-assessment. Perfectionists often impose unrealistic standards on people and tend to judge themselves harshly for minor errors.

3. Obsessive rumination and seeking reassurance: Many perfectionists experience obsessive thoughts about past failures or future goals. To deal with their anxiousness, they would constantly look to others for confirmation of their value and competence. However, some perfectionists hate receiving negative feedback because they are so terrified of it.

4. Overemphasis on achievements: Perfectionists often derive their feelings of worth from external performance standards, such as career advancement or academic standing. When one's high standards are not met, shame, guilt, and feelings of inadequacy can be very strong. This overemphasis on achievements may distort their self-perception, and they may develop a persistent fear of failing in all facets of their lives.

Recognizing these traits of perfectionism is the first step toward cultivating a healthier relationship with oneself and others. It is essential to strive for personal growth and excellence without succumbing to the paralyzing grip of perfectionism.

Perfectionism and Its Impact

Although commonly seen as a positive attribute, perfectionism can yield significant adverse effects in daily life. Research indicates that individuals exhibiting perfectionistic tendencies often experience elevated stress, diminished psychological well-being, and decreased life satisfaction. Perfectionism can impede various crucial facets of everyday existence when not properly addressed.

- Time management: Despite the apparent desire for perfection, research has linked perfectionism to self-sabotage behaviors such as procrastination and poor time management. Compulsive thinkers and failure-phobics may put off beginning a task they detest or take longer than required. Additionally, perfectionism can lead to a fear of trying new things, decreased creativity, and heightened self-doubt.

- Connection: Perfectionism can make it difficult to maintain fulfilling relationships. Family members may grow irritated with criticism, workaholic habits, or an unceasing need for validation and assurance.

- Stress levels: Perfectionists often experience burnout, overextension, and distress over time. Research shows that high degrees of perfectionism lead to much higher stress levels.

- Overall well-being: Chronic stress and a lack of self-care can raise the risk of mental health problems like anxiety and depression, as well as physical ailments like chronic fatigue syndrome (CFS).

Perfectionism has numerous negative repercussions on daily life. To maintain a happy and healthy existence, it is critical to understand its detrimental impacts and take action to address and manage its effects.

Characteristics of Perfectionism in Relationships

Perfectionism in relationships can cast a cloud over the most precious of bonds, transforming moments of intimacy and delight into battlegrounds of unreachable standards and unmet expectations. Here is how this never-ending desire for perfection can undermine the very foundation of love:

- A continuous state of overthinking: Every action and word is a potential minefield. Instead of appreciating the spontaneity of love, you are gripped by the fear of deviating from your well-constructed plan.

- Comparison to unrealistic expectations: You compare your relationship to an imaginary one you made up based on glimpses into the lives of others, forgetting that everyone has their own challenges and imperfections behind closed doors.

- Criticism reigns supreme: Rather than nurturing and supporting your partner, you constantly scrutinize their every move, holding them to impossibly high standards that you yourself struggle to reach.

- Maintaining mental scorecards: Every mistake, every error, is saved in the back of your mind, ready to be used as a shot in the next dispute or as a reminder of their perceived flaws.

- Discord equals failure: Rather than perceiving disagreement as a chance for growth and understanding, you see it as a harsh condemnation of the relationship's underlying defects, trapping you in a cycle of blame and anger.

- Lack of compromise and communication: In your pursuit of perfection, you lose sight of the fundamental elements of a healthy relationship: compromise and open communication. Vulnerability is viewed as weakness, whereas compromises are regarded as surrender.

- Dwelling only on the negative: In your constant endeavor to achieve perfection, you ignore fleeting moments of joy and connection, instead focusing on every perceived failure and defect.

- Avoidance results in isolation: Fearful of revealing your vulnerabilities to others' judgment, you retreat from social circles and intimate gatherings, depriving yourself and your partner of the rewarding experiences of shared connections.

- Honeymoon phase as the standard: Unable to reconcile the exhilarating thrill of new love with the constant tenderness of a long-term commitment, you cling to the honeymoon phase's ecstasy, pursuing an unsustainable high.

- Procrastination paralyzes progress: Your fear of failure leads to procrastination, delaying important conversations and milestones in the hope that perfection will magically materialize if you wait long enough.

Ultimately, perfectionism in relationships is not about achieving an unattainable standard of excellence; it is about recognizing and embracing the beautiful messiness of love—the flaws, the imperfections, and the moments of grace that make it all worthwhile. It is about learning to love not despite our humanity but because of it.

How to Overcome Perfectionism in Relationships

It would help to have an empathetic and understanding attitude when managing a relationship with a perfectionist. Both partners need to develop a curiosity about one another's personal lives, understanding that the perfectionist's stubbornness stems from previous hurt and feelings of unworthiness. By nurturing empathy, you can establish an emotionally secure environment where neither party constantly feels pressured to seek approval and love.

- Become curious and foster understanding: Cultivate curiosity about each other's inner worlds. Recognize that the perfectionists' rigid standards and fear of mistakes stem from deep-rooted experiences and emotions. Understand that perfectionists may have difficulty letting others in due to past hurts. Encourage open communication and create a safe space where you can both share your thoughts and feelings without judgment.

- Practice compassion: Be kind and understanding to one another. Recognize that each individual has coping strategies influenced by their past. Try to grasp that your value is not exclusively dependent on the degree of success you accomplish. Provide comfort and assurance to one another, proving that love and a relationship do not require perfection.

- Establish clear boundaries: Communicate and set boundaries to establish mutual respect and understanding. Discuss the kinds of behaviors that are appropriate and inappropriate in a partnership. When boundaries are broken, encourage open communication so that you can both constructively express your feelings and concerns.

- Celebrate achievements: Acknowledge and celebrate accomplishments and milestones, no matter how tiny. Encourage each other to celebrate one another's successes instead of focusing on imperfections. Celebrate your and your partner's achievements to cultivate a supportive and encouraging relationship culture.

- Take emotional risks: Be willing to share your vulnerabilities and take emotional chances. Step outside your comfort zone and encourage yourself and your partner to express your true feelings and desires. Create a supportive environment where you can freely express your innermost thoughts and feelings without fear of judgment. By tackling emotional risks together, you can develop and strengthen your relationship.

How Perfectionism Can Cause Anxiety

Imagine living in a society where every task, conversation, and moment is scrutinized through the lens of unattainable perfection. For many perfectionists, this is the reality, and unfortunately, it fosters anxiety.

Perfectionism is all about attaching your entire sense of value to reaching those standards; it is not simply about having high expectations. It is similar to balancing on a tightrope and constantly worrying that one mistake will cause you to fall into a well of failure and unworthiness.

It makes sense. The constant pressure to perform well and be exemplary can be oppressive. Each stumble feels like a betrayal of your identity, a personal failing (Matejko, 2022). The urge to prove your worth to both the outside world and yourself grows along with the worry.

The trouble is that aiming for perfection is like chasing a mirage in a deserted place. No matter how much you achieve or how many accolades you receive, it will never be enough. You find yourself in a perpetual cycle of self-doubt and anxiety since there is always more to achieve and more standards to meet.

Not to mention how anxiety exacerbates perfectionism, resulting in a vicious cycle that is difficult to escape. Anxiety is exacerbated by the worry of falling short of your own impossible standards, which then prompts even more compulsive thoughts and actions.

That need not be the case, however. There is so much more to you than your accomplishments, triumphs, and apparent shortcomings. The fact that you exist, imperfections and all, makes you worthwhile. Liberating yourself from the clutches of worry and perfectionism begins with accepting your flaws and allowing yourself to be human.

So be gentle with yourself. Practice kindness and self-compassion, particularly when the voice of perfectionism seems to be the loudest. Remind yourself that it is okay to fail sometimes and make mistakes. We grow, mature, and eventually bloom in this way.

If you ever find yourself struggling with overwhelming worry, it is important to remember that you are not alone. There are people who care about you and want to help, whether it is family, friends, a counselor, or a support group. Embracing your true self and finding solace in your imperfections is essential. Do not let anxiety and the pursuit of perfection hold you back from living a fulfilling life. Seek support and acceptance to help you through challenging times.

How to Stop Anxiety Intruding on Decisions

Picture a situation where your partnership is at a turning point, requiring you to make a decision that could impact the trajectory of your shared future. However, instead of leaving you feeling confident and logical, anxiety seeps in, clouding your judgment and entangling you in uncertainty. Does this sound familiar to you? Here is how to prevent relationship decisions from being influenced by anxiety (Younf, 2021):

- Bolster your brain's resistance to anxiety: Think of mindfulness as a personal coach for your brain. It helps strengthen the part of your mind responsible for making logical decisions, similar to how going to the gym strengthens your body. You can make wiser, more relationship-savvy decisions by tuning out distractions and focusing on what truly matters.

- Identify the true source of your anxiety: Take a moment to investigate. What is causing your anxiety? Is it work stress, past heartaches, or just the daily routine? Understanding where it comes from can reduce its impact and stop it from affecting your relationship.

- Slow it down: Although life moves quickly, you do not have to rush your decisions. Take a moment to pause and step out of autopilot mode. Pay attention to your emotions and the present moment. By slowing down, you can better understand your feelings and make thoughtful choices.

- Do not believe that thoughts, feelings, and behavior always go together: Just because anxiety shows up does not mean you have to entertain it. Challenge the norm and consider different reactions.

Remember, thoughts, feelings, and actions influence each other but are not inseparable.

- Fake it till you make it: Imagine yourself on a tightrope, carefully balancing between decisions. Anxiety is present, waving its arms and shouting warnings, but you do not have to listen. Instead, pretend that everything is fine. It may feel like you are faking it at first, but the more you practice, the easier it becomes.

- Just because there are choices does not mean there is a wrong one:

Release the pressure to pick the perfect path. Life is not a multiple-choice test with a right answer. Trust yourself to navigate the twists and turns, knowing there is no wrong turn—just different adventures waiting to unfold.

- Be guided by what you desire, not what you wish to avoid: Change the focus from fear to desire. Concentrate on what you want rather than what you are attempting to avoid. Allow your aspirations and ambitions to guide you, bringing your connection closer to happier places.

In the complex process of making decisions in a relationship, anxiety often tries to take center stage. However, by practicing mindfulness, self-awareness, and courage, you can outsmart anxiety and lead your relationship with confidence and clarity.

Exercise

Let's examine the possible causes of your perfectionism. Take out a pen and paper, and let's get started:

- Family and cultural influence: When you look back on your upbringing, take some time to consider whether perfectionism was valued or encouraged in your family or culture. How was the idea of perfectionism portrayed or reinforced? Were high standards expected, and how were they communicated or enforced?

- Response to mistakes and expectations: Recall a time from your childhood when you made a mistake. How did the adults around you react? Were they understanding and supportive, or did they respond with harsh criticism or punishment? Reflect on how these reactions shaped your views on failure and the pursuit of perfection.

- Parenting style: Consider your parents' parenting style. Did they follow one of the four parenting styles contributing to perfectionism (authoritarian, authoritative, permissive, or neglectful)? How did their approach affect your development and perception of perfectionism?

- Attention, validation, and pleasing others: Consider how you may have used perfectionism to get other people's attention, affirmation, or acceptance. Have you ever felt pressured to meet others' expectations or please them to avoid criticism? How did this pattern manifest in your behavior?

- Other contributing factors: Reflect on any other influences or events that might have influenced your perfectionism. Examine important life experiences, cultural influences, or personal convictions that might have influenced the development of your perfectionistic inclinations.

- Advice to your younger self: If you could go back in time and offer guidance to your younger self during moments of fear, anxiety, and self-doubt, what advice and comfort would you provide? Consider the empathy and support you would extend to help someone navigate the challenges stemming from perfectionism.

Spend enough time answering each question to allow you to explore your feelings and ideas further. This exercise in introspection and self-discovery will bring you insight into the causes of your perfectionism and point you in the right direction toward a kind and accepting future of who you are.

As we have explored the intricacies of overcoming perfectionism to enhance relationship satisfaction, another critical aspect awaits our attention: trust. Trust forms the bedrock of any healthy relationship, yet unresolved trust issues can erode connections and breed insecurity for many. The next chapter will delve into the journey of repairing and rebuilding trust, offering insights and strategies to foster deeper, more fulfilling connections with your partner.

Mid-Book Reflection: Share Your Thoughts

Thank you for joining me on this journey to transform your relationships and find freedom from overthinking. By now, you've explored key insights and tools to shift your mindset and build deeper connections.

If you've found something helpful or thought-provoking so far, I'd love to hear from you. Your thoughts could encourage someone else, just like you, to take the first step toward clarity, peace, and emotional intimacy.

There's no need to overthink your review—just speak from the heart. A few honest words about how this book has helped you can inspire others to begin their own journey.

Leaving a quick review is simple and makes a difference.
Use the QR code below or visit this link:

Your feedback helps others discover this resource and begin their own transformation. Thank you for being part of this meaningful process.

With gratitude,

Maria Elaina Paswell

6.
Unlocking Trust: The Secrets to Building a Healthy, Strong Bond

Sometimes, you cannot believe what you see; you have to believe what you feel. And if you are ever going to have other people trust you, you must feel that you can trust them, too—even when you are in the dark. Even when you are falling.

–Mitch Albom

What Are Trust Issues?

Trust is fragile. It is like a delicate glass sculpture that you painstakingly create over time, only to have it destroyed by someone with a single, powerful stroke. After it breaks, the pieces are never the same.

Trust is more than simply an idea found in self-help material. It serves as the binding agent in our connections. It makes us feel vulnerable, safe, and a part of the community. However, when that confidence is betrayed, it feels as though the earth beneath us is suddenly unsteady. We begin to doubt everyone and everything, wondering if they can really earn our trust.

Let's face it: Problems with trust are more than just a minor annoyance. They loom over every part of our lives like an unrelenting storm cloud. They permeate our thoughts, making us constantly question ourselves and other people. We become highly watchful, continually searching for indications of dishonesty or betrayal.

Living with persistent distrust and doubt is exhausting. It feels like carrying a heavy burden that never gets lighter. Worse, it can weaken the foundation of our relationships, causing us to push others away out of fear of being hurt again if we let them get too close

The issue is that trust issues aren't just about other people; they also affect us. They can distort our view of the world because they stem from our own fears and past painful experiences. Breaking free from their grip can be challenging. It demands vulnerability, courage, and a lot of self-reflection.

Struggling to trust others is common and a natural part of life. Rebuilding trust and fostering stronger, longer-lasting relationships is achievable through time, patience, and faith. While the process won't be simple, it is important to remember that nothing truly valuable comes without its challenges.

What Causes Trust Issues?

The complexities of trust issues arise from the intersection of our current circumstances and past traumatic experiences. These are not fleeting emotions; they impact all aspects of our lives. Recognizing their origins is the initial step to freeing ourselves from their grip.

1. Trauma: Trauma instills mistrust in us and leaves lasting wounds. It is hard to believe that we will not be hurt again after experiencing damage. Mental health practitioners recognize the importance of establishing trust with trauma survivors because they understand that safety is crucial for healing.

2. Hurtful childhood: Childhood is meant to be a period of carefree joy and wonder, yet for far too many, it is overshadowed by painful experiences that leave lasting scars. Whether enduring prolonged mistreatment or facing harmful behaviors, these wounds fester, sowing seeds of distrust that take root in our hearts. Studies indicate that the extent of childhood maltreatment is directly linked to the depth of distrust we carry into our adult lives.

3. Past relationship experiences: Betrayal cuts deep, leaving scars that affect our ability to trust again. Whether it is infidelity or unexpected betrayals, these experiences fracture the foundation of trust we build with others. Studies reveal that those who have experienced betrayal trauma struggle to trust not only romantic partners but also people in general.

4. Attachment style: The connections we establish during our formative years impact how we approach relationships in adulthood. When our emotional needs are not adequately met in childhood, it can lead to the development of insecure attachment styles. These attachment styles, characterized by feelings of uncertainty and mistrust, can significantly influence our behaviors and attitudes in romantic relationships. Research suggests that individuals with insecure attachment styles are more likely to experience heightened levels of distrust in their romantic relationships, which may manifest in behaviors such as possessiveness, suspicion, and emotional manipulation.

5. Mental health disorders: Mental health significantly affects our trust in others. Conditions like PTSD and anxiety disorders can amplify paranoia, making it hard to establish trust. Despite this, everyday trust is shaped by familiarity and confidence in our environment. Recognizing the origins of our trust issues and seeking support can help cultivate healthier relationships.

Types of Trust Issues in a Relationship

Relationship trust problems can take many forms, each of which illustrates the difficulties people encounter while trusting others. Even the most loving of relationships can be hampered by these problems, which range from the never-ending worry of infidelity to the incessant scrutinizing of a partner's words and behavior. However, the first step in resolving and gaining clarity is realizing the various kinds and degrees of trust concerns (Krueger, 2023).

1. Pistanthrophobia: A fear that damages trust by causing persistent anxiety about depending on other people, especially in romantic relationships. People who suffer from pistanthrophobia experience excessive and illogical fear, often in the absence of any real danger. They may struggle with perceived risks in their relationships, leading to avoidance or distancing behaviors.

2. Jealousy: Jealousy is on the other extreme of the emotional spectrum. It is a powerful feeling that leads to distrust and insecurity. People prone to envy have difficulty accepting other people in their partner's life because they see them as potential threats. This jealousy can lead to strained trust between partners, manifested through controlling behavior, possessiveness, or even outbursts of rage.

3. Fault-finding focus: Some people focus on what is wrong instead of right, distorting their perception of their relationships. They are overly critical and quick to point out their partner's flaws, making it hard for them to believe in their relationship's potential. Their lack of trust may not be based on specific actions but rather a pervasive sense of doubt that affects how they see things.

4. Self-doubt dilemma: In this case, people struggle with self-doubt and confusion about their own decisions, which causes the mistrust to be internal rather than external. They constantly second-guess themselves, wondering if there might be more appealing options elsewhere, driven by the dread of making the wrong choice. This perpetual sense of discontent can erode the foundation of trust within a relationship, leaving both partners feeling adrift.

Different types of trust issues can create unique and complex challenges, straining the relationship and the individuals involved. Despite this, it is important to understand that experiencing trust issues doesn't necessarily mean the end of a partnership. By openly acknowledging these issues and collaborating to resolve them with empathy and insight, couples can pave the way for healing and a stronger, more profound connection.

What Are the Signs of Trust Issues?

Recognizing signs of trust issues within yourself or your partner is crucial for fostering a healthy and fulfilling relationship. Here are some behaviors to watch out for:

1. Suspicion: Constantly doubting a partner's intentions, whereabouts, or actions without justification indicates underlying distrust, eroding the foundation of trust in the relationship.

2. Assuming the worst: Individuals with trust issues often assume the worst, such as interpreting a partner's lateness as a sign of infidelity rather than considering reasonable explanations like traffic or work delays.

3. Self-sabotage: Actions that hurt a relationship can stem from emotional distress and a fear of vulnerability. These actions include pushing your partner away during an argument, avoiding deep emotional connections, or ending the relationship early to protect yourself from potential pain in the future.

4. Grudge holding: People with difficulty trusting often hold on to past wrongs, whether committed by others or themselves. This refusal to forgive perpetuates old wounds and hinders the growth of relationships and personal development.

5. Negative focus: Trust issues can distort perception, causing individuals to fixate on the negative aspects of the relationship while disregarding the positive. This skewed viewpoint can overshadow moments of joy and connection.

6. Unfounded accusations: More often than not, psychological anxieties, rather than concrete proof, cause false accusations against a partner for alleged transgressions such as adultery or dishonesty. These unfounded assertions undermine mutual trust and create discontent in the partnership.

7. Anxious tendencies: Ongoing relationship concerns can lead to feelings of anxiety, paranoia, or even panic attacks, which can have a significant impact on overall relationships, physical health, and mental well-being.

8. Avoidant behaviors: Seeking emotional protection by avoiding deep connections, shying away from long-term commitments, or

keeping secrets can indicate trust issues. These avoidance tactics hinder intimacy and relationship growth.

9. Seeking validation: Constantly seeking reassurance or validation from your partner can create a cycle of dependency that strains both parties. This neediness can lead to unnecessary disagreements and discomfort, further exacerbating trust issues.

By recognizing these signs and addressing them with open communication, empathy, and possibly professional support, individuals can begin to heal and rebuild trust within their relationships.

Benefits of Trust

The foundation of every happy and fulfilling relationship is trust. It is woven into the fundamental fabric of a partnership together with openness, vulnerability, honesty, and respect. When words and deeds flow seamlessly, misgivings about motives are eliminated, and trust is established. It guarantees that what is stated is true and that what is promised will occur.

Trust, a fundamental element of any relationship, is not impervious to cracks. Due to human nature's inherent flaws, mistakes are bound to occur, often leading to breaches of trust. How these breaches are addressed and resolved plays a pivotal role in determining the partnership's resilience. Acts of kindness, meaningful changes in behavior, and genuine apologies serve as the adhesive that delicately pieces together and fortifies the trust within the partnership.

In relationships, trust is essential for the following five powerful reasons:

- Reassurance: Trust provides a sturdy foundation that reassures partners of their unwavering commitment to each other. Even amidst disagreements or conflicts, the trust in the relationship remains steadfast, offering solace that the bond is resilient enough to weather any storm.

- Healing: Trust is a soothing remedy for wounds caused by misunderstandings, unmet expectations, or hurtful actions. With trust, partners can navigate through pain, fostering forgiveness and healing.

- Foundation for love: Love flourishes in the fertile soil of trust. It serves as an anchor for love, offering stability and security. When there is trust, each person feels secure in their ability to depend on one another through difficult times, which nurtures the development of love.

- Overcoming complications: In a relationship, when both partners have a strong sense of trust in each other's consistent and unwavering support, they are better equipped to address and overcome challenges and obstacles that they encounter together. When there is trust, obstacles like diversity and challenges become opportunities for development and closer connection rather than unbreakable confines.

- Space and independence: When partners can offer each other the room and freedom to grow as individuals, trust liberates them. There is no place for mistrust or insecurity in a relationship based on trust; instead, partners feel safe letting each other follow their passions and interests without worrying about the other.

Trust is an essential element of a partnership and the relationship itself. The unseen thread links hearts between individuals and stimulates intimacy, growth, and steadfast support. Couples who work at building trust in their relationships can create a lasting link that enriches both of their lives profoundly.

How to Overcome Trust Issues in Your Relationship

Resolving trust issues can be complex and challenging. Still, it is possible to mend breaches and cultivate stronger, more wholesome relationships with dedication and effort. It involves open and honest communication, empathy, and a commitment to rebuilding trust over time. This journey requires patience, understanding, and a willingness to work through difficult emotions. Here is a roadmap to help you along the way:

- Embrace the risk: Accept that placing your faith in someone else exposes you to vulnerability and the possibility of disappointment. Recognize that nobody is flawless and that disappointment is a given. Establish clear expectations and boundaries while managing relationships.

- Understand trust dynamics: Everyone operates differently in terms of trust. Some trust instinctively, while others require trust to be earned. It is okay to take your time and allow individuals to prove themselves trustworthy, especially if you have experienced betrayal.

- Take emotional risks: Despite past hurts, courageously allow yourself to be vulnerable and choose to trust again. Whether at the beginning of a new relationship or after someone has proven themselves, taking emotional risks is essential for building genuine connections.

- Uncover the root cause: Delve into your past to understand the origins of your trust issues. Reflect on past betrayals or experiences that may have contributed to your apprehensions. Seeking the guidance of a counselor can provide invaluable insight and support in this process of self-discovery.

- Communicate openly: Foster honest and frequent communication with those in your life. Share your hesitations and concerns about trust openly, fostering understanding and transparency in your relationships.

- Mind your interactions: Pay attention to the dynamics of your interactions with others. Consider why specific people in your life might have earned your trust, and assess the trustworthiness of new people coming into your life.

- Value trusted relationships: Show that you are grateful to loved ones who have continuously helped you. Acknowledge the importance of trustworthy connections and their part in your life.

- Remain persistent and have faith in yourself: Never give up or second guess yourself in the face of obstacles or doubts. All experiences— good or bad— help you develop resilience and self-awareness.

Following these steps while staying committed to the process will allow you to overcome trust issues and create deeper, more meaningful relationships based on trust and understanding.

Exercise

Welcome to this trust-building exercise designed to help you address and overcome trust issues. Take a moment to focus on each step and reflect honestly. Let's get started:

1. Self-reflection: Think about specific past experiences that have affected your ability to trust. Jot down a few key events or situations. Then, consider how these experiences have impacted your trust in yourself, others, and the world around you.

2. Defining trust gaps: List out any specific trust deficits you have identified. Think about how these deficits show up in your life. Be clear and specific about how trust issues manifest for you.

3. Impact evaluation: Consider how these trust concerns have impacted your relationships, daily life, and overall well-being. Write down any instances where trust issues have significantly impacted your life.

4. Goal-setting: Set achievable goals to rebuild trust in yourself, those around you, and the world. Consider short-term and long-term objectives and express them clearly and feasibly.

5. Action plan: Create a clear and detailed action plan outlining the specific objectives of fostering trust. For each goal, specify a timeframe for completion, describe the actions you will take to achieve the goal, and list the resources you will utilize to support your efforts.

6. Seeking support: When working on rebuilding trust, reaching out to individuals or seeking resources to provide the support you need is crucial. This can include friends, family members, counselors, support groups, or other trusted individuals. By sharing your specific goals and action plan with them, you can create a robust support network to help you stay focused and motivated as you navigate rebuilding trust.

7. Review and adapt: Review your progress regularly and adjust your goals and action plan. Remember, healing takes time, so be patient with yourself and stay committed to the process.

Take your time with each step of this exercise, and remember to approach it with compassion and honesty. Trust-building is a journey, and every small step forward counts.

Understanding that addressing and resolving trust issues is only the first step in a complex process is crucial. While it is essential to work through these issues, it is equally important to actively maintain trust to enrich the depth and quality of your relationships. In the upcoming chapter, we will explore in detail the strategies for building trust and nurturing and sustaining it. These insights will lay the groundwork for fostering happier, more fulfilling relationships.

7.
Investing in Your Relationship to Achieve Emotional Balance

We have to recognize that there cannot be relationships unless there is commitment, unless there is loyalty, unless there is love, patience, and persistence.

—Cornel West

Emotional Investment

Understanding emotional involvement in relationships requires recognizing the depth of care and commitment. It surpasses mere attraction or curiosity, evolving into a mutual investment akin to placing trust in a project for emotional fulfillment. Like financial investment, emotional investment expects reciprocity: love, understanding, and support in return. Genuine commitment involves caring for your partner's feelings and prioritizing open communication to address conflicts. Quality time together is not just a want but a necessity, reinforcing the bond and fostering mutual growth.

Emotional investment requires respecting boundaries and showing genuine interest in your partner. It fosters understanding and respect, making each person feel valued. However, commitment is not easy. Past relationship trauma or fears can hinder full emotional commitment, and vulnerability can lead to uncertainty or a fear of rejection when opening up to someone new.

Furthermore, picking up on signs of codependency or unhealthy behavior in a partner may trigger caution in emotional investment, leading to doubts about the relationship's longevity. Strong emotional investment entails a deep commitment to fostering a happy, healthy bond. Each individual must tread this path with mindfulness and self-awareness, addressing past concerns and traumas while nurturing respect and understanding within the relationship.

Things to Consider Before Investing Your Emotions Into a Relationship

Engaging in a relationship with someone you feel something for is a significant step that can impact your future and general well-being. While having a deep connection to someone is common, it is crucial to proceed carefully and thoughtfully while making such commitments. Before investing all of your energy into a relationship, remember the following:

- Assess your level of preparedness: Dealing with the risks and weaknesses that accompany emotionally investing in someone requires readiness. Think about whether you are prepared to face the risks and challenges that may arise. Understand that you have no control over a situation once emotions become involved. Make sure your mind and emotions are up to the task at hand.

- Emotional reciprocity: Determining whether the other person shares your feelings is essential. Investing in someone you're not emotionally compatible with can lead to disappointment and pain. Before committing fully, take the time to understand their feelings.

- Consider your limits: As much as partnerships need compromise, preserving your distinctiveness and boundaries is important. Consider how much you can compromise without completely losing who you are. Respect for each other's needs and autonomy is essential to the success of healthy relationships. By being aware of your boundaries, you can avoid making excessive sacrifices and endangering your mental health.

- Evaluate their value in your life: Consider whether they positively impact your life and whether their absence would significantly affect your happiness. Invest in someone who makes you feel good about yourself rather than settling for someone who does not see your value.

- Trustworthiness: Any connection starts with trust. Make sure the person you are emotionally investing in is reliable and considerate of your emotions. Heartbreak and betrayal can result from a lack of trust. Spend time observing their honesty, sincerity, and dedication to developing a genuine relationship.

- Independence and happiness: Developing a sense of contentment and happiness within yourself before making an emotional commitment is essential. It is important to continue nurturing these feelings. When you are content with your own company, you are not seeking validation or happiness solely from the relationship.

Cherishing your independence and focusing on your personal growth and happiness are crucial. You cannot fully love and emotionally engage with someone else unless you are comfortable and confident in your own skin.

It is normal to feel deeply connected to someone in a relationship. Still, it is crucial to approach it with mindfulness and self-awareness. Building healthy and meaningful relationships involves considering personal readiness, mutual feelings, setting and respecting boundaries, valuing the other person, trust, and individual fulfillment.

Remember, taking care of your emotional well-being should be a top priority.

How to Strengthen Your Relationship With Your Partner

When aiming to strengthen the bond with your partner, thinking of your relationship as a bank account can be helpful. Just like managing a financial account, the interactions and experiences you share with your partner can be seen as either deposits or withdrawals. Positive actions, thoughtful gestures, and effective communication can be considered deposits, building up the emotional balance within your relationship. Conversely, negative interactions, misunderstandings, and hurtful behaviors can be seen as withdrawals, potentially depleting the emotional reserves within your relationship. By being mindful of the impact of your actions and interactions, you can work towards maintaining a healthy and balanced emotional account with your partner.

Drawing from the Gottmans' insights, couples who consistently prioritize turning toward each other tend to cultivate greater long-term happiness (Saluja, 2018). These acts of emotional investment, or deposits, signify interest, care, and active engagement in nurturing the relationship.

Here are some tips for strengthening your relationship bank account:

- Replace criticism with positivity: Make a conscious effort to draw attention to and recognize your partner's accomplishments rather than focusing on their flaws. Enhancing their positive traits makes them more appreciative and builds trust.

- Express gratitude: Encourage an environment of appreciation by consistently thanking your partner for their accomplishments and positive traits. Small acts of acknowledgment can lead to a stronger sense of connectedness.

- Lead with empathy: Practice understanding and listening with empathy. By considering your partner's emotions, you can strengthen your emotional bond and affirm their experiences. Genuine curiosity and concern for their feelings strengthen the bond.

- Respond to emotional prompts: Always remember to respond favorably when your partner tries to connect or offer assistance. Establishing mutual trust and demonstrating empathy and unity strengthens your commitment to the partnership.

Every relationship has struggles, but emphasizing fulfilling conversations and emotional connection can significantly increase its resiliency and vibrancy. By making deliberate investments in your relationship's bank account, you may strengthen your relationship with your partner and improve your sense of emotional fulfillment.

Emotional Bank Account

The concept of the emotional bank account provides a clear framework for managing emotional dynamics in relationships. Similar to a real bank account, deposits and withdrawals influence the balance. A zero or negative balance signals issues. Responding positively to your partner's emotional bids adds to the account while ignoring them and withdrawing from it. Many studies highlight that successful couples prioritize turning toward each other, making emotional deposits more frequently than withdrawals.

One key finding from a six-year study of newlywed couples underscores this principle: Compared to those who divorced, those who stayed married showed a noticeably higher rate of accepting their partner's attempts for emotional connection (Dollard, 2018). This difference in behavior reflects the crucial role that managing the emotional bank account plays in relationship satisfaction and longevity.

So, how do you gauge the balance of your Emotional Bank Account? Enter the 5:1 ratio, a simple yet powerful guideline for maintaining a healthy emotional connection:

1. Focus on deposits: Couples must prioritize increasing deposits (positive interactions) while minimizing withdrawals (negative interactions) to foster satisfaction in the relationship.

2. During conflict: Aim for a ratio of five positive interactions to every one negative interaction. This ensures that even amid disagreements, the overall emotional balance remains positive.

3. In everyday life: Strive for an even higher ratio of twenty positive interactions to every one negative interaction. Everyday interactions carry significant weight in shaping the emotional landscape of the relationship.

Reframing conflict resolution involves prioritizing positive interactions over being agreeable. Turning toward your partner, actively listening, validating their perspective, and expressing empathy contribute to positive interactions amid disagreements. Negative interactions act as significant withdrawals from the emotional bank account, emphasizing the need for prioritizing positive habits daily. Cultivating an emotionally rich relationship relies on consistent, small deposits rather than grand gestures. Couples sustain a fulfilling connection by nurturing positive interactions and minimizing withdrawals, enriching their Emotional Bank Account over time.

How to Invest in Your Emotional Bank Account

Investing in your emotional bank account and strengthening your emotional bond with your partner requires deliberate effort and mindfulness. You can enhance your connection and fortify your bond by incorporating specific behaviors into your daily interactions.

Investing in your emotional bank account can be done in these ways:

- Engage in mindfulness: Practice being present and noticing what is happening around you. Notice your partner's emotional clues and attempts to establish a connection. Actively turn toward them, showing that you value and acknowledge their emotional needs. While you may not catch every prompt, the more you prioritize these positive interactions, the easier it becomes to recognize and respond to them.

- Express daily appreciation: Take time each day to reflect on how your partner has shown care and support. Whether it is a simple text message or a shared moment while completing household tasks, express gratitude for these gestures of connection. Cultivating a positive perspective fosters a culture of appreciation within the relationship.

- Discuss stress together: Acknowledge and address external stressors that may impact your relationship. Set aside time for stress-reducing conversations, allowing each partner to express their feelings and experiences without focusing on marital issues. Emphasize understanding and validation of your partner's perspective to strengthen emotional intimacy.

- Communicate understanding: When your partner shares their frustrations or joys, focus on understanding rather than problem-solving. Express empathy and validate their emotions, demonstrating that you hear and accept their feelings. Building this reciprocal emotional connection fosters a sense of love and support within the relationship.

- Be physically affectionate: Physical touch, such as kissing, holding hands, and cuddling, serves as an opportunity to deposit into your emotional bank account. The Normal Bar study highlights the importance of physical affection in maintaining a fulfilling relationship (Northrup et al., 2014). Make time for affectionate gestures to reinforce your emotional connection.

By starting small and consistently investing in your emotional bank account, you can gradually strengthen the bond with your partner. One by one, these positive interactions sculpt a relationship characterized by love, respect, and emotional intimacy.

Maintain a Positive Balance in Your Emotional Bank Account

Make significant deposits as much as possible while reducing withdrawals to keep your emotional bank account in positive balance and build a healthy connection. Here is how to strike this equilibrium:

Making Deposits

Positive interactions and behaviors that build our relationships contribute to the emotional bank account. These might be as basic as showing gratitude, paying close attention, offering help, or just spending time with those who are dear to you. Through regular practice of these behaviors, we strengthen emotional closeness, enhance communication, and build trust.

- Make an effort to understand them: Be genuinely interested in your partner's goals, viewpoints, and experiences. Connect with them by putting yourself in their position and developing empathy.

- Pay attention to the small things: Show consideration and decency with small, kind gestures. Acts of kindness, polite words, and well-mannered behavior show your partner how much you value and care about them.

- Maintain your promises and commitments: Keep your word to your partner. Building trust and reaffirming the dependability of your relationship requires consistency and reliability in your activities.

- Set clear expectations: It is important to openly communicate your boundaries and expectations with your partner and yourself. Take the time to be mindful and ensure everyone clearly understands each other's boundaries and expectations. This can help prevent misunderstandings and confrontations in the future.

- Show personal integrity: Be honest and genuine in all that you do. Let your actions reflect the values and principles you believe in, showing your partner that you are trustworthy and authentic. Lead by example, demonstrating integrity and reliability in every aspect of your relationship.

- Apologize when necessary: Acknowledge your mistakes and take responsibility for any withdrawals you have made. Offer genuine apologies and commit to making amends, rebuilding trust and connection.

Minimizing Withdrawals

Just like with real-life bank accounts, our emotional bank accounts run on empty if we keep taking out of them as time goes on without adding to them. Withdrawals include actions that damage a relationship of trust, like lying, breaking commitments, being careless, or showing a lack of empathy. These behaviors cause animosity, emotional distance, and sometimes even the relationship's collapse.

- Keep your word: Make an effort to honor your commitments and avoid making unrealistic promises. Establishing trust and stability in the partnership requires consistent dependability.

- Practice kindness: In all your interactions, it is essential to be mindful of the impact of your words and actions. Choose to approach situations with compassion and empathy rather than hatred or judgment. You create a positive and encouraging atmosphere by respecting your partner and fostering a healthy and fulfilling relationship.

- Respect expectations: Adhere to the limits and standards established in the partnership. Crossing these boundaries damages trust, and resentment and conflict may result.

- Avoid blame and defensiveness: Encourage open communication by refraining from accusing or defensive actions. Instead, handle disagreements with compassion and an open mind to one another's points of view.

- Make connection a priority: Ignoring your partner's emotional needs or running from meaningful discussions can result in emotional distance and frustration. To strengthen your relationship, prioritize emotional closeness and quality time.

You can cultivate a relationship marked by mutual respect, trust, and emotional fulfillment by intentionally making deposits and limiting withdrawals in your emotional bank account. To protect the health and vitality of your relationship, check the balance in your account regularly and make any necessary adjustments.

Key Messages

1. Approach relationships with intention: People vary in their openness and trust levels. Some naturally radiate positivity, while others may take time to build trust. It is essential to approach every relationship with the intention of making regular trust deposits through your words and actions. This approach fosters a foundation of trust and positivity, regardless of individual differences.

2. Understand different perspectives: Different perspectives can lead to a rich and diverse exchange of ideas. It is important to remember that everyone's viewpoint is shaped by their unique experiences and beliefs. Embracing these differences can lead to more well-rounded discussions and a deeper understanding of various topics. However, overanalyzing relationships based on preconceived notions can lead to stress and misunderstandings. It is essential to approach interactions with an open mind and a willingness to understand others' points of view.

3. Build a positive balance: Putting money into your emotional bank account builds a trust reserve resilient to occasional withdrawals. By regularly placing deposits of positivity and trust, you strengthen

your relationships' resilience. Keeping a healthy balance in your emotional bank ensures the relationship stays solid and encouraging, even during bad days or trying times.

Why Some People Are Afraid to Invest Their Emotions in a Relationship

Many individuals harbor an underlying fear of intimacy, manifesting as a subconscious aversion to closeness in personal relationships. This fear, whether of physical or emotional intimacy, often surfaces within our closest and most significant connections.

Apprehension and distrust toward love often stem from fears of rejection, relationship decline, or unreciprocated affection. Paradoxically, our fear of intimacy can be triggered by positive emotions more than negative ones. Being chosen by someone we sincerely care for and experiencing their affection can evoke profound intimacy fears, complicating maintaining close relationships.

Ironically, the primary resistance to intimacy does not typically stem from the actions of our partners but rather from an internal opponent lurking within us. The discrepancy between our partner's positive perception of us and the negative self-image we carry on our own creates inner conflict. Unfortunately, we cling to our negative self-perceptions, resistant to accepting a different view of ourselves. Consequently, it becomes challenging for us to allow the reality of being loved to impact our core self-image, leading to resistance to love.

These negative core beliefs, often rooted in childhood experiences, characterize us as fundamentally flawed, unlovable, or deficient. Although these beliefs may be distressing, they are familiar and ingrained in our subconscious. As adults, we mistakenly perceive these beliefs as fixed and impossible to alter.

We often unintentionally reject love in our efforts to preserve a sense of familiarity and identity. This can occur during moments of closeness and intimacy when our instinctive reactions lead to behaviors that create friction in the relationship. As a result, we inadvertently drive our loved ones away despite our genuine desire for connection and closeness.

Many people distance themselves emotionally due to a fear of intimacy, often fueled by overthinking. They include:

- Holding back affection: They might doubt their partner's intentions or worry about getting hurt, so they keep their feelings to themselves.

- Reacting poorly to praise or affection: A person may react unfavorably or not at all because they believe their partner is being deceitful or attempting to control them.

- Developing paranoia or suspicion: One may begin to read too much into situations and overanalyze their partner's behavior, which can lead to feelings of distrust or suspicion.

- Losing interest in intimacy: People who overthink things tend to worry excessively about their relationships or performance, disrupting their mood and making them less interested in intimacy.

- Being unjustly critical: They may concentrate excessively on their partner's shortcomings and errors, resulting in unrelenting criticism and nitpicking.

- Avoiding closeness: People who overthink situations and worry about being wounded often build emotional barriers and avoid becoming overly attached to their partners.

How to Recognize a One-Sided Relationship and Restore the Balance

When you were in a relationship, did you ever feel like you were the only one trying? That is what we call a one-sided relationship. It happens when one person seems to be carrying all the weight while the other goes along for the ride, creating an imbalance.

A healthy partnership is distinguished by mutual support and equality. You both understand that you can count on one another, and you each provide a fair contribution. It is comparable to having a solid base to build a strong connection.

In contrast, a one-sided connection is different. Ultimately, one person bears the burden—emotionally, financially, or in other ways. For instance, in a romantic relationship, one partner may start the conversation, organize special occasions, or handle duties that must be divided equally.

One-sided relationships can be difficult because they make you feel exhausted and undervalued. You may wonder if the other person is genuinely grateful for what you have done for them or if they are merely seeking to take advantage of you.

Recognize that creating and maintaining healthy, fulfilling relationships requires effort and cooperation from both partners. Suppose you find yourself consistently shouldering most of the responsibilities. In that case, initiating an open and honest conversation with your partner is essential to address the imbalance. In a mutually supportive relationship, both partners should be equally committed to each other's well-being and success, striving to create a harmonious and balanced partnership.

Common Signs of Imbalance

Identifying the warning signals of an unbalanced relationship is critical to keeping your happiness and well-being. Red flags to watch out for include the following:

- You initiate most activities and conversations: You often initiate discussions and activities, while the other person seldom takes the lead or contributes to planning shared experiences.

- Navigating important decisions solo: You often take the lead in significant relationship choices, as the other person appears disinterested or unwilling to shoulder responsibility for them.

- Bearing the apology burden: Following disagreements, it is usually you who extends the olive branch and makes an effort to mend fences, while the other party remains silent or sidesteps their role in the conflict.

- Compromising personal needs: The other person's well-being takes precedence over your desires, leading you to prioritize their happiness to sustain the bond.

- Anxiety and uncertainty: Their apparent lack of investment leaves you feeling unsettled and skeptical about your standing in the relationship, creating doubts about their level of commitment and intentions.

- Communication roadblocks: Conversations often feel lopsided, with minimal interest or comprehension from the other party. Despite your efforts to connect, you frequently walk away feeling unheard and dissatisfied.

- Financial disparities: In shared expenses, most of the responsibility falls on your shoulders. Additionally, there is a possibility that the other party may turn to you to address their financial obligations, effectively adding strain to your financial situation.

- Frequent justifications: You often make excuses for the other person's lack of contribution, attributing it to their stress or bad mood. However, these justifications do not prevent them from behaving carelessly.

Recognizing these signs is the first step toward addressing imbalances in your relationship and fostering healthier dynamics. Prioritizing your well-being and seeking support to navigate these challenges is essential.

Are One-Sided Relationships Worth Fixing?

One-sided relationships prompt reflection on their potential for repair. Social psychologists suggest sacrificing for someone you love demonstrates care and fosters positive self-perception. Indeed, acts of selflessness can generate feelings of fulfillment and strengthen bonds. However, research also indicates a caveat: caution is warranted if one consistently finds oneself in the role of the sacrificial giver or if sacrifices feel coerced (Gordon, 2012).

It is crucial to grasp the fundamental dynamics at play. Is the one-sidedness a result of temporary circumstances or deep-seated differences? Clear and open communication is of utmost importance in this situation. Engaging in honest dialogue about needs, expectations, and concerns can shed light on ways to achieve balance. However, if one party consistently ignores the needs of the other, reestablishing trust and fairness may present significant challenges.

Reciprocity, the practice of exchanging things with others for mutual benefit, is an essential aspect of healthy relationships. It involves a balanced give-and-take dynamic where each person contributes to the well-being and happiness of the other. When reciprocity is absent in a relationship, it can lead to feelings of imbalance and resentment

In addition to reciprocity, self-awareness is crucial in maintaining healthy relationships. Self-awareness involves recognizing and understanding one's thoughts, emotions, and behaviors. It also means establishing and maintaining personal boundaries and having a solid sense of self-worth. This self-awareness enables individuals to stand up for fair treatment and identify when a relationship becomes toxic, empowering them to decide to walk away if necessary.

The choice to invest in healing a one-sided relationship ultimately comes down to how committed each party is to growth and transformation. Although giving up something for someone you love can be honorable, your well-being should not suffer. Maintaining long-lasting and satisfying partnerships requires finding a balance between giving and receiving.

What About a Partner Who Does Not Want to Change?

When faced with a situation where a partner seems unwilling to change, several factors must be considered before deciding on the next steps. Research indicates that it is important to question whether your partner has demonstrated a similar level of commitment and is undergoing a similar thought process (Gordon, 2012).

Evaluate your partner's input: Carefully consider the specific behavior or trait your partner is unwilling to change. Reflect on whether it is an integral part of their personality or a pattern that could potentially be altered with dedicated effort. Understanding the deep-rooted reasons behind this behavior and gauging the level of adaptability required is vital for making well-informed decisions in your relationship.

Consider the context of your relationship: Have you respectfully and clearly expressed your wishes and concerns? Good communication lays the groundwork for mutual understanding and compromise. However, more significant issues may arise if your significant other avoids having an open conversation with you or minimizes your concerns.

Assess the overall give-and-take balance in the partnership: Are you constantly making compromises while your partner refuses to budge? A healthy partnership requires mutual respect, support, and reciprocation. If one partner consistently refuses to make concessions, it can lead to disharmony and resentment.

Evaluate your values and boundaries: Are you sacrificing your health or morality to persuade your partner to change? Recognizing and respecting your needs is crucial to maintain your mental well-being and self-worth.

At some point, you may need to reassess the strength of your relationship if your partner is unwilling to change, and the dynamics are upsetting or unsatisfactory. While change is natural for individuals, relationships cannot endure without mutual respect and a shared commitment to growth. If your loved one is unwilling to compromise, it may be time to prioritize your own happiness and well-being.

How to End Things

Knowing when to walk away from a relationship is a crucial decision that requires careful consideration. It becomes especially important when your partner is unwilling to compromise, leading to persistent conflicts and unhappiness. Despite the effort and dedication you may have invested in the relationship, there are instances where the compatibility and mutual understanding necessary for a healthy connection are simply not present. In such cases, prioritizing your emotional well-being becomes paramount, even though taking this step may be emotionally challenging.

Be honest: When it comes to ending a relationship or discussing difficult topics, it is crucial to communicate with honesty and sensitivity. Explaining your reasons without assigning blame is essential for maintaining respect and understanding. Using "I" statements allows you to express your feelings and needs without being critical or judgmental. It is perfectly acceptable to articulate your desires for future expectations or deeper personal connections, as these factors can pave the way for meaningful and constructive conversations.

Consult a therapist: Consider seeking support from a therapist to help you heal from the breakup and gain insight into your role in the unhealthy relationship. Exploring deep-seated attitudes or behaviors, such as codependency or people-pleasing, can pave the way for healthier and more satisfying relationships in the future.

Take time to heal: Even if you have decided to end a relationship for the sake of your own well-being, it is completely normal to experience feelings of sadness and confusion. It is important to understand that prioritizing your own needs doesn't diminish the love you may still feel for your partner. This healing period requires self-care, introspection, and a willingness to confront your emotions to move forward.

Without equality and mutual respect, relationships can become strained and emotionally taxing. If efforts to address imbalance are unsuccessful, it may be necessary to acknowledge the incompatibility and make the difficult decision to end things for the sake of your own happiness and fulfillment.

Exercise

The cornerstone of any healthy relationship is trust. Couples rely on it to stay together through thick and thin, much like glue. However, trust is a quality that develops over time; it doesn't just appear magically. The ten simple yet effective activities listed below are designed to nurture trust between partners. These activities are helpful strategies for improving and enhancing your relationship with your partner. By incorporating these activities into your relationship, you can strengthen your bond and grow closer, building a solid foundation of trust.

Offer space and privacy: Resist the temptation to constantly check in on your significant other. Instead, intentionally offer them the space and privacy they need to perform their activities undisturbed.

Opportunities for building trust: Let your partner show that they are trustworthy by letting them handle tasks on their own or make decisions without constant supervision.

Exchange information: Exchange personal details and facts about each other in turn. Throughout the process, ensure each partner feels valued and at ease; never force or coerce sharing.

Exercise eye contact: To deepen intimacy and connection, spend extended periods gazing into each other's eyes, progressively increasing the duration.

Physical boundaries conversation: After an open discussion about physical boundaries, spend uninterrupted time cuddling while respecting those boundaries. Then, discuss the experience and address any issues that may arise.

Exercise communication: Take turns speaking for five minutes, during which the other partner must listen without interrupting. After that, talk about the experience and take turns in your roles as the speaker and listener.

Obstacle course: Put on a blindfold and lead your companion through an obstacle course to help them develop confidence in your guidance and their capacity to depend on you.

Reminisce: Remember and discuss pleasant memories you have had together to reinforce good feelings and shared experiences.

Mixtape: Create personalized playlists and share them with each other. Curate a collection of songs that hold special meaning or express your feelings for each other. Share the music that resonates with your emotions and experiences.

Weekly sessions: It is important to schedule a regular weekly session to openly communicate your plans and responsibilities, express gratitude, and address any ongoing concerns or difficulties you might be facing. These frequent check-ins will help us stay aligned, accountable, and supportive in our partnership, ensuring that you are on the same page and working together effectively.

Now that we have explored various effective strategies for investing in relationships, it is important to understand that these efforts have a cumulative impact over time. While nurturing your connection with your partner is crucial, it is equally vital to continue investing in your self-esteem. Doing so will strengthen your sense of worth and confidence, which will help you remain resilient in the face of challenges within your relationship. The upcoming chapter will thoroughly explore practical methods to cultivate and sustain healthy self-esteem. This will empower you to navigate your relationships with clarity, confidence, and assurance.

Securing Your Identity

8.
Elevating Your Self-Worth by Building Confidence and Esteem

The greatest thing in the world is to know how to belong to oneself.
—Michel de Montaigne

The Difference Between Self-Confidence and Self-Esteem

Self-confidence and self-esteem are crucial for perceiving yourself and interacting with the world. Although they may appear similar, their subtle differences impact your sense of self and experiences.

Simply put, self-confidence is the belief in your abilities and traits. It reflects your mindset about overcoming challenges, achieving goals, and adapting to various situations. For example, self-confidence is evident when you feel comfortable performing live and have faith in your musical abilities. It is something you develop through repetition, interactions, and encouraging feedback.

Now, self-esteem goes deeper. It is the recognition of your inherent value and dignity, independent of achievements or external validation. Self-esteem is the unshakable belief that you are valuable simply because you exist. Someone with high self-esteem respects themselves, recognizes their intrinsic value, and approaches life with resilience and openness.

Think of self-confidence as the outward expression of your abilities and skills to others. Self-esteem, however, is more internal. It's about how you perceive your value regardless of outside influences.

These two aspects can influence each other. For instance, you may be confident in certain areas yet still experience feelings of unworthiness. Conversely, cultivating strong self-esteem can help you sustain and grow your confidence. The key to a content and fulfilling life is balancing self-confidence with self-esteem—embracing your intrinsic value while also believing in your ability to face life's challenges.

How Low Self-Confidence and Self-Esteem Can Lead to Overthinking

Low self-confidence and low self-esteem can trigger excessive overthinking. In a culture that often equates success with personal value, fear of failure or rejection can create a loop of self-doubt and rumination. This cycle may lead to overanalyzing past actions, decisions, and potential outcomes.

n relationships, these tendencies can manifest in various ways. Someone with low self-esteem might constantly question their partner's love or loyalty, scrutinizing every interaction for signs of abandonment.

Similarly, those with low confidence may doubt their ability to be a good partner, leading to overthinking their words and actions in an effort to avoid rejection or criticism.

Low self-esteem and confidence often result in feelings of vulnerability and insecurity in relationships, increasing the likelihood of misunderstandings, tension, and unnecessary conflict. Breaking this cycle requires recognizing these patterns and working to build both confidence and self-esteem.

Signs You Have Low Self-Esteem and Self-Confidence

If you are noticing signs of low self-esteem or self-confidence in yourself, it is vital to recognize how they might be showing up in your life:

Low Self-Esteem

- Self-criticism: Constantly being unreasonably critical of yourself while fixating on perceived flaws and weaknesses and ignoring strengths.

- Feelings of inferiority: Comparing yourself unfavorably to others.

- Negative self-talk: Having a persistent inner monologue that undermines your value.

- Lack of self-recognition: Struggling to take credit for your own achievements.

- Self-blame: An inclination to take blame even when you have no control over it.

- Disbelief in compliments: Struggling to accept or believe positive feedback or praise.

Low Confidence

- Self-doubt: Constant uncertainty or hesitation regarding your abilities and decisions.

- Passive behavior: Often taking a backseat in social situations or avoiding asserting your opinion.

- Difficulty trusting others: Struggling to trust or rely on others' judgment or intentions.

- Inferiority complex: Feeling like you don't measure up to others' standards.

- Sensitivity to criticism: Overacting to feedback or perceiving it as a personal attack.

- Feelings of unworthiness: A strong and unwavering belief that you do not deserve love, care, or success.

Building higher self-esteem and confidence starts with recognizing these telltale signs. Remember, if you need help navigating these emotions, it is okay to ask friends, family, or a professional for support.

Causes of Low Self-Confidence and Low Self-Esteem

Understanding factors contributing to poor self-esteem and confidence is critical for personal development. Here are a few key aspects to think about (Markway, 2018):

1. Past trauma: Being physically, sexually, or emotionally abused can significantly impact your self-worth. Traumatic memories and emotions may linger, affecting various aspects of your life.

2. Parental influence: The treatment you receive as a child from your parents or other caregivers can have a long-lasting impact. Growing up with persistent criticism, comparisons to others, or dismissive attitudes might bring self-doubt and feelings of inadequacy as an adult.

3. Bullying and harassment: Experiencing emotional trauma as a result of bullying as a child or harassment as an adult can be permanent. Over time, negative experiences with one's appearance, skills, or social interactions can damage a person's self-confidence and self-worth.

4. Social pressures: One's opinion of oneself can be influenced by societal norms surrounding gender, race, and sexual orientation. Feelings of inadequacy or self-doubt may become internalized due to discrimination or stereotyping.

5. Negative authority figures: Self-confidence can be damaged by criticism or disapproval from parents, teachers, or employers, among other authority figures. Unrealistic expectations or relentless pessimism can breed a never-ending feeling of worthlessness or failure.

6. Cultural and religious beliefs: Cultural or religious beliefs that uphold rigid norms, shame, or guilt can impact self-esteem. These ideas may cause one to feel sinful or inadequate, leading to internal struggle and self-criticism.

7. Media influence: Self-esteem may be impacted by media representations of cultural norms and unattainable beauty standards. Persistent exposure to idealized representations and comparisons to unachievable benchmarks might exacerbate emotions of inadequacy or self-dissatisfaction.

The events of the past do not determine your future and value. Even though negative perceptions may have affected your self-worth, you can challenge and overcome them. It is essential to know that you are not alone in your struggles.

You can regain your confidence and self-esteem by surrounding yourself with positive people, seeking help, and practicing self-compassion. Embrace and appreciate the journey of self-discovery and growth you are on, understanding that the first step to building resilience and improving your self-worth is identifying the root of your low self-esteem. With time and effort, you can develop a healthier relationship with yourself and deserve to feel worthy and capable.

How to Build Self-Confidence and Self-Esteem

Building self-confidence means setting out on a meaningful path of personal development. It is essential to understand that every person's journey to building confidence is different, and it is okay to go at your own pace, taking baby steps at first before taking bolder ones.

- Accept your individual path: Making unjustified comparisons to others might result in self-doubt. Remember that your value does not depend on other people's accomplishments. Take breaks from social media when necessary, as it can serve as an epicenter for comparison. Celebrating your progress at your own pace is good because your journey is uniquely yours.

- Celebrate your wins: Acknowledging and celebrating every victory is crucial for personal growth and well-being, no matter how small. Whether you conquer your fears or simply engage in positive self-talk, each achievement deserves recognition. Taking the time to appreciate your successes builds resilience and boosts self-confidence. By embracing and celebrating every triumph, you create a positive and empowering mindset that can propel you forward in the face of adversity.

- Adopt a growth mindset: Embrace challenges as opportunities for learning and growth. Understand that failure is just a stepping stone towards success, not the end. Use the lessons you learn from failures to propel yourself forward.

- Step outside comfort zones: Growth happens when you stretch yourself. Take on the challenge of taking risks and embracing new experiences. Every step outside your comfort zone increases your confidence and strengthens your skills.

- Practice self-compassion: Treat yourself with kindness and respect. Positive self-talk and affirmations can help you develop a supportive inner dialogue. Recognize your own strengths and values to reinforce that you deserve love and success.

- Set healthy boundaries: To protect your well-being, set boundaries in your interactions. Decide what is appropriate for you and express it with confidence. Prioritize what you need and develop the capacity to say no when needed to safeguard your emotional well-being and self-esteem.

- Surround yourself with positivity: Build a positive and supportive circle of people around you. Let go of unhealthy relationships that make you feel insecure and seek approval from others. Being in the company of positive people creates a space to grow and build confidence.

- Build curiosity: Welcome curiosity as a means of achieving reflection and self-realization. Experience a sense of fulfillment and purpose as you explore new interests and passions.

- Let go of the people-pleasing mentality: Move your focus away from pleasing others and toward your well-being. Establish boundaries that respect your needs and ideals, and learn to say no without feeling guilty.

Look for inspirational resources: Read books, follow accounts on social media, or tune into podcasts that encourage a sense of confidence and personal growth to improve your knowledge and perspective.

Keep in mind that developing self-confidence is a process rather than a destination. While you overcome obstacles and acknowledge your accomplishments, practice self-compassion and patience. You can create a strong feeling of self-assurance and lead an authentic life consistent with your goals and ideals.

How Do You Build Self-Esteem and Confidence in a Relationship?

When our confidence in the relationship and ourselves wanes, we may exhibit behavior that jeopardizes the relationship. To help your relationship feel more confident, think about using these tactics (Davenport, 2023):

- Prioritize yourself: Self-love is the foundation of a wholesome relationship. Caring for your physical, mental, and emotional well-being takes commitment and work. Make conscious nutritional decisions, integrate daily affirmations into your routine, and schedule downtime for reflection and relaxation. You will observe that your confidence in the relationship grows naturally as you take care of your sense of worth.

- Release past baggage: Although past experiences have shaped us, they do not have to control our current relationships. Fully embrace the present by letting go of past wounds and heartaches. While it is essential to acknowledge the lessons learned from past relationships, it is equally crucial not to let them overshadow your current connection.

- Establish relationship expectations: Mutual understanding and harmony can only be achieved by setting clear expectations in your relationship. Communicate with your partner honestly and openly, expressing your needs and wants without passing judgment or throwing accusations. Open and honest conversation increases confidence in the relationship and fosters trust.

- Embrace friendship: Priority should be given to establishing a solid foundation of friendship in your relationship. Cultivate laughter, trust, and meaningful experiences with your partner to deepen emotional intimacy. Friendship is a catalyst for building confidence and nurturing a secure bond with your partner.

- Authenticity reigns: Be unapologetically yourself within the relationship. Embrace your individuality and express your desires openly and honestly. Authenticity breeds confidence and fosters a genuine connection with your partner.

- Dress confidently: Take pride in your appearance and choose attire that expresses who you are and reflects your self-assurance. While physical appearance is not everything, presenting yourself confidently can positively impact your self-confidence within the relationship.

- Honor personal space: Acknowledge the significance of individual autonomy and personal boundaries in your relationship. Allow your partner the freedom to pursue their interests and activities independently. Respecting each other's space fosters trust and confidence in your ability to maintain independence within the relationship.

- Nurture independence: Strengthen your friendships, pursue your interests, and work for your objectives to help you feel independent outside of your relationship. Embracing your independence increases your self-esteem and lessens the need for romantic fulfillment alone.

- Positive communication: When speaking with your partner, avoid blaming and criticizing them. Instead, emphasize cooperative problem-solving and positive communication. Relationship satisfaction increases when both parties feel appreciated and respected in a supportive environment.

- Avoid relationship tests: Do not put your relationship to the test or use deceptive methods to get approval. Have faith in the foundation of your relationship and communicate honestly with your partner about any worries or insecurities you may have.

Implementing these tactics into your relationship can help you develop self-confidence and strengthen your bond with your partner. Recognize that growing confidence in a relationship is a process that calls for tolerance, candid communication, and respect for one another.

Exercise

The following activity is intended to help you develop self-worth and strengthen your relationships. This exercise will examine how valuing oneself is linked to cultivating fulfilling relationships with others. By thinking about your personality traits, behavior, and goals, you will discover the beauty of self-appreciation and its significant influence on your relationships.

1. Find a peaceful, cozy area where you can concentrate without interruptions.

2. Breathe deeply for a few moments to help you center and focus on the here and now.

3. Read the affirmation: "Appreciating myself serves my relationships. When I love and value myself, I enhance the beauty of my connections with others."

4. Reflect on the following questions, allowing yourself to answer them honestly and thoughtfully:

    a. What are three qualities about myself that I admire and appreciate?

    b. How do these qualities positively contribute to my relationships with others?

    c. Think of a recent interaction with a loved one. How did I demonstrate kindness, understanding, or support in that interaction?

    d. How can I take care of myself first today to improve my relationships and well-being?

    e. How can I meaningfully show myself and my loved ones how much I appreciate and value them?

5. As you write down your answers to each question, take some time to consider your intentions, attitudes, and strengths regarding yourself and your relationship.

6. Consider your responses and recognize how vital self-love is to building happy relationships.

7. Commit to incorporating appreciation and self-care for yourself and your loved ones in your everyday routine.

8. As you wrap up the practice, express gratitude for the depth of your relationship and the beauty of your self-awareness.

Keep this feeling of gratitude close to you as you care for your connection with your partner and yourself.

After discussing the significance of developing a positive self-image, let's look at how this might improve communication with your partner. In the upcoming chapter, we will discuss simple strategies for communicating with clarity and conviction, which will help you build stronger relationships and create a more satisfying dynamic in your partnership.

Tailoring Your Communication Approach

9.
Empathy, Active Listening, and Vulnerability—Keys to Healthy Communication

Beliefs and assumptions drive the perception.
—STEVEN REDHEAD

How Poor Communication Can Lead to Overthinking and Vice Versa

Poor communication and overanalyzing often lead to a harmful cycle in romantic, familial, or friendship relationships. This pattern can be very damaging, causing more stress and strain on the partnership.

Ineffective communication within a relationship contributes to miscommunication, unsolved problems, and unfulfilled needs. Minor issues fester and become more significant sources of conflict when they could have been readily resolved with honest and transparent communication. As a result of this ineffective communication, one or both parties might read too much into circumstances, intentions, and motivations. When concerns are not clearly communicated or validated, people assume the worst and fill in the blanks with their interpretations.

Overthinking can worsen communication issues. When individuals become too absorbed in their own perceptions and fears, they may fail to express themselves adequately or avoid communicating altogether out of fear of being misunderstood or rejected. This reluctance to speak honestly further strains the relationship, forming a cycle of faulty communication and overanalysis.

In toxic relationships, the cycle of negative behavior can become particularly relentless and damaging. Power struggles, emotional abuse, and manipulative actions are prevalent in toxic dynamics. They can significantly contribute to elevated stress and anxiety levels. In such situations, individuals may feel an intensified need to overanalyze and overthink their circumstances for self-protection and survival.

It takes a concentrated effort to address underlying issues causing overthinking and enhance communication skills to break away from this loop. It also requires creating an environment of understanding, empathy, and trust within the partnership. This can be accomplished by actively listening, being honest and transparent about one's feelings, and validating one another's experiences.

One should focus on overcoming one's tendency to overthink. This may involve actively challenging negative thought patterns and acknowledging how past traumas or insecurities contribute to overthinking behaviors. Self-reflection, journaling, or therapy can help develop improved coping mechanisms and gain insight into one's mental processes.

Ultimately, escaping this harmful cycle and creating happier, more satisfying relationships is possible by prioritizing open and truthful communication and resolving the root causes of overthinking.

What Constitutes Poor Communication

Poor communication can take various forms, eroding relationships and contributing to stress and tension between individuals. Here are some key examples:

1. Not genuinely listening: This type of inadequate communication occurs when one fails to pay attention to and understand the other person actively. It can manifest in various ways:

    a. Lazy listening: This happens when someone seems to be listening but isn't engaged or attentive. They might just respond with something like "uh-huh" instead of paying attention to what the other person is saying. Even while it might seem innocent, it could compromise the quality of the relationship and give the speaker a sense of devaluation.

    b. Waiting to respond: In this scenario, one person is more focused on formulating their response than listening to their partner. They might steer the conversation in their direction or use it to advance their agenda, ultimately disrupting meaningful communication and impeding understanding.

    c. Refusing to listen: Ignoring or failing to consider the other person's perspective may be the most harmful type of poor listening. This dismissive conduct can cause anger, contempt, and a sense of being ignored or irrelevant in the relationship.

d. Refusing to listen: Ignoring or failing to consider the other person's perspective may be the most harmful type of poor listening. This dismissive conduct can cause anger, contempt, and a sense of being ignored or irrelevant in the relationship.

2. Passive-aggressive communication: This style is characterized by subtly expressed anger or annoyance, frequently covered up by sarcasm or ingenuine agreeableness. For example, consider:

    a. Forgetting and denying: When one partner agrees to something, they may conveniently "forget" or "deny" their agreement afterward, which wears trust and creates uncertainty.

    b. Continuous disagreement: When individuals argue frequently about trivial matters, especially in public, it can cause stress and unease. It can be challenging to deal with passive-aggressive conduct head-on, which leaves one feeling helpless and frustrated.

3. Aggressive communication: This type of communication is characterized by overt hostility, criticism, or even verbal abuse. It can include:

    a. Criticism and name-calling: Individuals using aggressive communication tactics may attack the other person's character or actions to assert dominance rather than seek understanding.

    b. Hostility and conflict: Anger-based communication intensifies disputes and damages confidence, making it challenging to build solid connections or find a constructive way to settle disagreements.

Ineffective communication creates miscommunication, hatred, and conflict in relationships, which makes everyone unhappy and worn out. Addressing these communication problems requires attentive listening, empathy, and a readiness to have frank conversations. One can improve relationships and develop healthy communication practices by encouraging mutual respect and understanding.

Good Communication in a Relationship

In the realm of fostering healthy relationships, effective communication stands as a cornerstone. Both individuals involved must be willing to unveil aspects of themselves to each other, creating a space where openness thrives.

Fear often inhibits this exchange. Fear of rejection or concern over the partner's response can stifle the relationship's growth, hindering its potential.

The benefits of robust communication in relationships are manifold:

1. Fostering love: Love, like a delicate flower, requires nurturing to flourish. While initial infatuation may sustain some, it inevitably wanes. Honest communication serves as a reminder of the love's roots, fortifying the bond between partners.

2. Resolving misunderstandings: Discord often arises from differing perspectives. Effective communication bridges these gaps, fostering understanding and enabling conflict resolution.

3. Deepening understanding: True intimacy stems from knowing one another deeply. Communication is the vessel through which this understanding is cultivated, laying the groundwork for a profound connection.

4. Fostering respect: Respect is the bedrock of any healthy relationship. Effective communication elucidates boundaries and expectations, fostering mutual respect between partners.

5. Eliminating guesswork: Uncertainty breeds discord. Clear communication eradicates guesswork, promoting harmony and understanding.

6. Establishing trust: Openness and vulnerability are prerequisites for earning trust. This trust is built by regular, honest conversation, which provides a secure environment for both partners to confide in each other.

7. Offering support: It is easier to bear hardships when they are shared. Partners who communicate well can help one another during difficult times by being aware of each other's challenges.

8. Mood enhancement: Sincere communication promotes mental health. Open communication about happiness and sadness improves mood and deepens the connection between two people.

9. Strengthening the relationship: Communication is essential for the health of any relationship. Frequent communication encourages growth by enabling partners to discuss problems and share victories.

10. Encouraging learning: Every encounter presents a chance for improvement. When partners communicate openly, they can learn from each other and strengthen their bond.

Communication is the lifeblood of any relationship, serving as the conduit through which love, understanding, and growth flow. Its importance cannot be overstated; it is the foundation upon which healthy, enduring connections are built.

Signs a Relationship Has Healthy Communication

Understanding healthy communication in a relationship is essential to its development and longevity.

- Sincerity and kindness: Effective communicators are both sincere and compassionate. Being honest and forthcoming about emotions and perspectives is essential for this. Sincerity and empathy are both present in statements like "This is how it feels for me" or "This is how I see it from my perspective" (Mosemann, 2022).

- Body language: Be mindful of how your body language conveys your emotions and stances in a relationship. Effective communicators in partnerships lean in when speaking, displaying attentiveness and engagement.

- Fairness in speaking: Both partners in a healthy partnership can freely express their opinions. Communication should be two-way, with each partner sharing thoughts and feelings without fear of judgment or interruption.

- Kind and concise statements: Effective communication doesn't require verbosity. Partners should be able to convey their thoughts and emotions in a kind, brief, and straightforward manner. Directness fosters clarity and understanding.

- Expressing concerns with gratitude: While addressing concerns is essential, healthy communication involves framing them with appreciation and affection. Expressing gratitude before and after raising concerns demonstrates respect and consideration for the other person's feelings.

By recognizing these signs, individuals can assess and nurture the quality of communication within their relationships, fostering greater understanding, trust, and connection.

Things That Can Inhibit Good Communication

Effective communication is vital for developing a deeper connection and trust in a relationship. However, various barriers might obstruct the flow of communication, preventing the interchange of ideas, emotions, and experiences. Here are some frequent barriers to good communication:

- Misunderstandings: Misunderstandings can result from differences in interpreting or perceiving, which can break down communication.

- Limited shared interests: Mismatched interests can make finding common ground for meaningful communication challenging.

- Individual differences: Individuals with clashing personalities, values, or backgrounds may struggle to comprehend and communicate with each other.

- Arrogance and self-focus: A self-centered approach to communication can drown out the other person's needs and perspectives, suppressing genuine interactions.

- Judgmental attitudes: Making harsh judgments or criticisms might prevent free communication and vulnerability.

- Defensiveness: Reacting aggressively to feedback or criticism can inhibit effective communication and problem-solving.

- Guilting into forgiving: Invalidating someone's sentiments or experiences by forcing them to forgive or forget can erode trust and prevent communication.

- Inconsistent physical language and communication: Nonverbal indicators that contradict verbal communication may result in uncertainty and distrust.

- Cowardice or aversion to tough challenges: Fear of confrontation or unpleasantness can cause people to avoid important subjects, hindering resolution and understanding.

- Unregulated anger: Anger or animosity can aggravate disagreements and impede good communication.

- Failure to keep promises: Breaking commitments or neglecting to follow through on promises can undermine confidence and create communication barriers.

The first step in recognizing and overcoming these obstacles is acknowledging their existence. Seeking help from a licensed expert, such as a therapist, can provide counsel and strategies for enhancing communication within the relationship. With both partners' willingness and effort, means of communication can be restored and strengthened, enabling deeper connection and understanding.

The Importance of Emotional Awareness in Communication

Emotions are crucial in all relationships and serve as the foundation of communication. Being emotionally aware, which involves recognizing and understanding feelings, is vital for effective communication. When you are emotionally aware, your communication skills significantly improve. You become more attuned to the emotions of others, understanding how their feelings impact their communication. Additionally, you gain insight into the underlying messages conveyed by others, comprehending what is said and why it is said.

Consider a situation where someone is upset yet unable to express their feelings. Being emotionally aware allows you to detect their pain through subtle indications in their voice, mannerisms, or choice of words. Understanding their emotional condition enables you to respond with empathy and compassion, making a more meaningful connection.

Trying to hide emotions is generally useless since emotions emerge despite our efforts to ignore them. Rather than curbing or denying feelings, growing emotional awareness entails acknowledging and accepting them. By refining this skill, you improve your ability to navigate the complex landscape of human emotions, resulting in more genuine and meaningful interactions in relationships.

How to Communicate Better in a Relationship to Stop Overthinking

Improving communication in a relationship to alleviate overthinking requires intentional steps:

- Establish communication guidelines: Outline how you both approach communication as a couple. Having clear guidelines fosters a sense of security and understanding.

- Encourage openness: Establish an environment where both partners feel comfortable expressing themselves without worrying about criticism or negative consequences.

- Speak kindly: Prevent harsh criticism that might exacerbate tense situations by approaching conversations with kindness and empathy.

- Employ "I" statements: Instead of blaming or pointing fingers, begin conversations by expressing your emotions. Use words like "I feel" to express your feelings without using accusatory statements or placing blame.

- Understand before responding: Try to grasp your partner's point of view before answering, rather than treating conversations as arguments. Don't listen to respond. Listen to understand. Pay attention, and don't let winning the argument consume you.

- Control your emotions: Give yourself some time to relax and gather your thoughts before starting a conversation. This will ensure that discussions remain productive instead of turning into heated arguments.

- Self-reflection: Take the time to understand your own emotions and triggers before addressing issues with your partner. This self-awareness helps you communicate more effectively and manage conflicts constructively.

- Prioritize compromise and resolution: Make compromise and resolution the goal of communication. Both partners should leave conversations feeling understood and validated, even if a complete agreement isn't reached.

- Release fear of division: Let go of the fear that communication may lead to division. Embrace the idea that healthy communication strengthens the bond between partners rather than causing rifts.

- Practice: Regularly practice effective communication strategies to reinforce positive communication habits and deepen connection in the relationship.

What to Do When Your Partner Is a Poor Communicator

Addressing poor communication with your partner requires tact and sensitivity. Rather than discussing it during a heated argument, broach the topic during a time of warmth and openness. Initiate a conversation about the communication dynamics in your relationship, emphasizing a desire for constructive dialogue.

Express your aspirations for healthier communication without resorting to criticism. Focus on articulating what you hope to achieve together, steering clear of blame or fault finding. Offer specific examples of how certain adjustments could benefit the relationship, such as explaining how raised voices may hinder your ability to process information.

Encourage your partner to share their perspective and any areas they believe could improve. Collaborate on establishing communication guidelines and developing strategies for implementing them during conflicts. Consider methods for grounding yourselves in these guidelines during heated moments, whether taking a pause to regroup or engaging in post-conflict discussions to reflect on communication strategies.

Approaching the issue with empathy and a willingness to collaborate fosters an environment conducive to growth and improvement in communication within the relationship.

Seven Active Listening Techniques

Active listening goes beyond hearing and involves actively absorbing and understanding the spoken words. Below are some ways to enhance your attentive listening skills:

- Remain fully present: Give the discussion your whole attention and engage fully. This entails paying attention to the speaker with all of your senses and putting the brakes on outside distractions.

- Recognize nonverbal cues: Body language and tone of voice can convey a lot about a person's intentions and emotions. If you pay close attention to these signs, you can understand the speaker's intentions and feelings more clearly.

- Maintain appropriate eye contact: Throughout the conversation, show that you are present and attentive by retaining appropriate eye contact. Try not to stare too much to minimize discomfort.

- Pose open-ended questions: Foster deeper dialogue by posing open-ended questions encouraging the speaker to elaborate and share more about their thoughts and feelings.

- Reflect on what you hear: Paraphrase or summarize the speaker's words to confirm understanding and validate their perspective. This illustrates listening intently and dispels any possible misunderstandings.

- Practice patience: Allow the speaker to express themselves fully without interruptions or premature responses. Do not rush the discussion or prepare your response while they are still speaking.

- Suspend judgment: Establish a judgment-free environment where your partner can talk freely without worrying about being judged or criticized. Practice acceptance and empathy to promote trust and understanding during communication.

Using these strategies for focused listening can improve your communication ability and build stronger relationships with people.

Exercise

In relationships, feeling blamed can often trigger defensiveness. This defensive reaction can hinder effective communication. One approach to mitigate this is to use "I" statements. These statements help individuals express their feelings and concerns without blaming their partner.

Example:

Blaming: You never help with the household chores! It's like I'm doing everything myself.

"I" statement: I feel overwhelmed when I do excessive housework. I could really use some help.

Now, let's delve into more scenarios where "I" statements can be applied. Fill in the blanks with your own "I" statements to address these scenarios effectively.:

Scenario 1: Your partner promised to attend an important event with you but backed out at the last minute. Recently, you were eagerly awaiting their presence at a family gathering when they called to say they couldn't make it.

"I" statement: _____

Scenario 2: Your partner frequently interrupts you when you're speaking during discussions or arguments.

"I" statement: _____

Scenario 3: Your significant other often forgets important dates, such as anniversaries or birthdays, which makes you feel unappreciated.

"I" statement: _____

Scenario 4: Your partner spends excessive amounts of time on their phone or other devices, neglecting quality time with you.

"I" statement: _____

Scenario 5: Your significant other criticizes your choices or actions in front of friends or family, embarrassing you.

"I" statement: _____

Fostering positive relationships hinges on effective communication. Healthy communication habits pave the way for meaningful and fulfilling connections with others.

Conclusion

It takes time and determination to overcome overthinking in relationships; change does not happen instantly. Instead, it occurs slowly and progressively. As you've reached the end of this book, you may realize that the strategies described here act as a road map, pointing toward happier relationships and a more satisfying life.

A crucial part of this process is realizing the power of positive thinking. By recognizing its tremendous impact on the state of mind and relationships, you prepare a path for change. Breaking free from self-defeating habits takes time and self-compassion. As you move through these changes, remember that you are growing and that every effort counts toward progress.

Communication lies at the heart of healthy relationships. Strengthening these skills is a continual practice that requires dedication and persistence. You actively combat overthinking and foster deeper connections by honing your ability to express concerns clearly and prevent assumptions.

Upon completing this book, you're equipped with a toolbox of strategies to recognize the root causes and triggers of overthinking, empowering you to make radical changes. Engaging in self-care practices and improving relationship quality enables you to manage stress, overcome perfectionism, and achieve a balanced emotional investment.

Moreover, securing your identity and boosting your self-confidence affirms your worth and lay the foundation for confident, fulfilling relationships. This book's ultimate objective is to support a profound metamorphosis toward empowerment, mental calmness, and the capacity to cultivate wholesome, healthy relationships.

As you set out on this rewarding adventure, never forget that you have the power to write the story of your relationships. With effort and perseverance, you can sense the deeply satisfying joy of fulfilling relationships and the tranquility of overcoming overthinking..........

Thank You for Coming on This Journey

Your decision to pick up this book was likely driven by a desire to find relief from the constant overthinking, self-doubt, or anxiety that has weighed on your relationships. By taking this journey, you've already started to transform those challenges into opportunities for growth, clarity, and connection.

Now, imagine sharing what you've gained with someone standing where you once were—overwhelmed by overthinking, searching for emotional balance, and longing for deeper, more authentic relationships. Your review could guide them to take the first step toward the peace and fulfillment you've begun to discover.

Take a moment to scan the QR code or visit the link below to share your thoughts. Together, we can inspire others to find their path to clarity, confidence, and connection.

With heartfelt gratitude,

Maria Elaina Paswell

References

Ahern, C. (2013). How to fall in love. HarperCollins UK.

Alade, T. (2022, February 27). How overthinking ruined my relationships and how I overcame it. Tiny Buddha. https://tinybuddha.com/blog/how-overthinkingruined-my-relationships-and-how-i-overcame-it/

Anwar, B. (2023, January 27). Self-Sabotaging relationships: Signs & causes. Talkspace. https://www.talkspace.com/blog/self-sabotaging-relationship/

Astahovskis, T. (2022, July 28). Am I problem-solving or overthinking? LinkedIn.

https://www.linkedin.com/pulse/am-i-problem-solving-overthinking-tomsastahovskis/

Austin, D. (2023, December 8). Relationship "tests" are all over social media. Couples therapists share which to trust. TODAY. https://www.today.com/health/viralrelationship-tests-couples-therapists-rcna128583

Ayivor, I. (2014). Leaders' watchwords. CreateSpace.

Bambora, Z. (2023, August 10). How to stop overthinking causes and symptoms of overthinking. HopeQure. https://www.hopequre.com/blogs/what-causesoverthinking-and-how-to-overcome-it

Barkley, S. (2023, December 1). How to forget something: 6 tips. Psych Central. https://psychcentral.com/health/how-to-forget-something#coping-tips

Becoming emotionally invested in A relationship- and setting healthy boundaries. (2024, March 10). Regain. https://www.regain.us/advice/general/when-do-you-become-emotionally-invested-in-a-relationship-learning-healthy-boundaries/

Bennett, R. T. (2020). The light in the heart: Inspirational thoughts for living your best life. Roy T. Bennett.

Bennett, T. (2022, August 16). Trust issues: Signs, causes, and how to overcome them. Thriveworks. https://thriveworks.com/blog/trust-issues/

Bethards, B. (2012). Sex and psychic energy. SCB Distributors.

Beyer, A. L. (2020, September 24). Do your relationships often seem to self-destruct? Figure out if you're the one who's been setting the clock. Greatist. https://greatist.com/grow/relationship-self-sabotage#roots-of-self-sabotage

Bhardwaj, N. (2021, January 8). Here are 4 ways in which overthinking is sabotaging your relationship. Healthshots. https://www.healthshots.com/mind/emotional-health/here-are-4-ways-in-which-overthinking-is-sabotaging-your-relationship/

Boles, E. (2020, November 16). How cognitive distortions can sabotage your relationship. Modern Intimacy. https://www.modernintimacy.com/howcognitive-distortions-can-sabotage-your-relationship/

Brown, A. D., & Mueller, J. (2023, August 1). What does it mean to be emotionally invested? WikiHow. https://www.wikihow.com/EmotionallyInvested#:~:text=Emotional%20investment%20happens%20when%20you

Cabral, C. (2020, April 3). Emotional bank account—6 examples for stronger relationships. Shortform Books. https://www.shortform.com/blog/emotional-bank-account-examples-7-habits/

Casabianca, S. S. (2013, December 26). Are obsessions a mental health symptom? Psych Central. https://psychcentral.com/blog/how-to-stop-obsessive-thoughts#letsrecap

Cherry, K. (2023a, November 7). Why you may have trust issues and how to overcome them. Verywell Mind. https://www.verywellmind.com/why-you-may-have-trustissues-and-how-to-overcome-them-5215390#toc-why-trust-issues-are-harmful

Cherry, K. (2023b, November 16). How to tell if you're in a one-sided relationship. Verywell Mind. https://www.verywellmind.com/one-sided-relationship-signscauses-effects-coping-5216120

Chung, M. (2022, January 6). How to fix trust issues in a relationship. Talkspace. https://www.talkspace.com/blog/trust-issues-in-a-relationship/

Clarke, J. (2023, November 25). Dealing with perfectionism in a relationship. Verywell Mind. https://www.verywellmind.com/dealing-with-perfectionism-in-arelationship-5226092#:~:text=Perfectionism

Cognitive distortions in relationships worksheet. (2022). https://happiertherapy.com/wp-content/uploads/Cognitive-Distortions-in-Relationships-worksheet.pdf

Cognitive distortions: Types, effects, & how to stop them? (2022, February 28). Therapy Mantra - Online Therapy Counseling. https://therapymantra.co/negativefeelings/cognitive-distortions/#How_Cognitive_Distortion_Affects_Life

Cole, C. (2022, November 28). A therapist explains 5 "thinking errors" that lead to overthinking. IntrovertDear. https://introvertdear.com/news/a-therapistexplains-5-thinking-errors-that-lead-to-overthinking/

Courtney, N. J. (2020, December 30). Trust in a relationship: Why it's important—and how to build it. The Healthy.

https://www.thehealthy.com/family/relationships/trust-in-a-relationship/

Cuncic, A. (2024, February 12). 7 active listening techniques for better communication.

Verywell Mind. https://www.verywellmind.com/what-is-active-listening3024343

Dalier, M. (2020, January 13). Overthinking and anxiety: Part 1. Georgetown Psychology. https://georgetownpsychology.com/2020/01/overthinking-andanxiety-part-1/

Das, T. (2023, September 11). Cognitive distortions that could be impacting your relationship. Hindustan Times.

https://www.hindustantimes.com/lifestyle/relationships/cognitive-distortions-that-could-be-impacting-your-relationship-101694421693642.html

Davenport, B. (2023, October 25). Lacking confidence in your relationship? 15 tips to empower yourself and feel self-assured. Live Bold and Bloom. https://liveboldandbloom.com/10/relationships/confidence-in-relationships#1how-to-be-confident in a-relationship-15-tips-to-feel-self-assured- de Montaigne, M. (1993). Michel de Montaigne: The complete essays. Penguin Books.

Dempsey, K. (2021, September 24). What is overthinking disorder? The Awareness Centre. https://theawarenesscentre.com/what-is-overthinking-disorder-does-itexist/

DeRossett, T. (2022, February 8). 5 signs of healthy communication in a relationship. Tidewater Physicians Multispecialty Group. https://www.mytpmg.com/5-signsof-healthy-communication-in-a-relationship/

Dollard, C. (2017, September 13). Invest in your relationship: The emotional bank account. The Gottman Institute. https://www.gottman.com/blog/investrelationship-emotional-bank-account/

Dorwart, L. (2023, September 19). Understanding the psychology behind perfectionism. Verywell Health. https://www.verywellhealth.com/perfectionism-5323816

Effects of overthinking on mental and physical health. (2021, February 25). Stree Sanman. https://www.streesanman.com/effects-of-overthinking-on-mental-andphysical-health/

Elsig, C. M. (2022, January 24). The dangers of suppressing emotions. The CALDA Clinic. https://caldaclinic.com/dangers-of-suppressing-emotions/

Erdrich, L. (2009). The last report on the miracles at little no horse. Harper Perennial.

Eurich, T. (2018, January 4). What self-awareness really is (and how to cultivate it). Harvard Business Review. https://hbr.org/2018/01/what-self-awareness-really-is-and-how-to-cultivate-it

Fletcher, L. (2023, January 9). The emotional bank account. Rightworks. https://www.rightworks.com/blog/the-emotional-bank-account/

Fournier, A. B. (2023, November 7). Are you sabotaging your relationships? Verywell Mind. https://www.verywellmind.com/are-you-sabotaging-your-relationship4705235#:~:text=Self

Fran. (2022, May 18). How to build confidence: 5 tips for being more confident. FutureLearn. https://www.futurelearn.com/info/blog/general/how-to-buildconfidence-5-tips-being-more-confident

Gallo, M. (2019, January 15). Council post: How to avoid the everyday thinking traps that sabotage your success. Forbes.

https://www.forbes.com/sites/forbescoachescouncil/2019/01/15/how-to-avoidthe-everyday-thinking-traps-that-sabotage-your-success/?

Gillette, H. (2019, October 31). Self-Sabotage in relationships: 10 signs. Psych Central.

https://psychcentral.com/relationships/the-startling-reason-we-sabotagelove#takeaway

Gillette, H. (2022, September 12). "Trust issues": Signs, causes, and how to overcome distrust. Psych Central. https://psychcentral.com/blog/trust-issues-causessigns#causes-of-lack-of-trust

Glass, L. J. (2019, January 22). Why is trust important in a relationship. Pivot.

https://www.lovetopivot.com/the-importance-of-trust-in-a-relationship/

Godreau, J. (2023, November 10). 8 unexpected reasons why perfectionism is bad for your mental health. Mindful Health Solutions.

https://mindfulhealthsolutions.com/8-unexpected-reasons-why-perfectionismis-bad-for-your-mental-health/

Goggin, M. E. (2023, June 23). How A lack of self-awareness in relationships can destroy the relationship. Free & Connected. https://freeandconnected.com/how-a-lackof-self-awareness-in-relationships-can-destroy-the-relationship/

Gonsalves, K. (2023, May 1). 12 ways to communicate better in relationships, from marriage therapists. Mind Body Green.

https://www.mindbodygreen.com/articles/how-to-communicate-better-inrelationships

Gordon, A. M. (2012, August 15). When are you sacrificing too much in your relationship? Greater Good.

https://greatergood.berkeley.edu/article/item/when_are_you_sacrificing_too_much_in_your_relationship

Gould, W. R. (2023, March 7). Why vulnerability in relationships is so important. Verywell Mind. https://www.verywellmind.com/why-vulnerability-inrelationships-is-so-important-5193728

Grande, D. (2021, February 2). When perfectionism harms you or your relationships. Psychology Today United Kingdom. https://www.psychologytoday.com/gb/blog/in-it-together/202102/whenperfectionism-harms-you-or-your-relationships

Gupta, A. (2022, April 29). Are you stuck in the vicious cycle of overthinking? It's risky, warns an expert. Healthshots. https://www.healthshots.com/mind/mentalhealth/heres-how-overthinking-can-impact-your-overall-health/

Gupta, S. (2023, December 6). How to build trust in a relationship. Verywell Mind. https://www.verywellmind.com/how-to-build-trust-in-a-relationship-5207611#:~:text=Increases%20Closeness

Habit 6: Emotional bank account. (2020, May 8). Flow Office Wisdom. https://www.flowofficewisdom.com/blog/3dqt2h6d36gn14xm09s9dgd44nm3b5

Hartney, E. (2023, November 8). 10 cognitive distortions that can lead to addiction relapse. Verywell Mind. https://www.verywellmind.com/ten-cognitivedistortions-identified-in-cbt-22412

Hooks, B., & West, C. (1992). Breaking bread: Insurgent black intellectual life. South End Press.

How perfectionism is linked to anxiety. (2021, May 18). UPMC HealthBeat. https://share.upmc.com/2021/05/perfectionism-linked-to-anxiety/

How to implement the practice of vulnerable communication. (2018, May 15). Toronto Caribbean Newspaper. https://torontocaribbean.com/how-to-implement-thepractice-of-vulnerable-communication/

How to overcome trust issues in relationships: signs & causes. (2024, January 11). Calm Blog. https://www.calm.com/blog/trust-issues

How to stop overthinking everything, always. (2023, August 24). Calm Blog. https://www.calm.com/blog/how-to-stop-overthinking#:~:text=Low

How to stop overthinking in a relationship. (2021, July 28). Mindwell NYC. https://mindwellnyc.com/how-to-stop-overthinking-in-a-relationship/

How to stop overthinking in a relationship - 5 tips and signs. (2023, July 17). Anchor Light Therapy Collective. https://anchorlighttherapy.com/overthinking-in-arelationship/

Huziej, M. (2023, November 27). All about cognitive distortions. CPD Online College. https://cpdonline.co.uk/knowledge-base/mental-health/cognitive-distortions/

"I" statements (worksheet). (2017, April 29). Therapist Aid. https://www.therapistaid.com/therapy-worksheet/i-statements

Identifying cognitive distortions in relationships. (2023, December 16). Cognitive Behavioral Therapy Los Angeles. https://cogbtherapy.com/cbt-blog/cognitive-distortions-in-relationships

Jalodara, D. (2024, February 27). The origins of overthinking. Medium. https://medium.com/@jalodaradhruv73/the-origins-of-overthinking3eaddde69873

Johnson, S. (2019, July 8). How using "I" statements in relationships can benefit you. Marriage Advice - Expert Marriage Tips & Advice. https://www.marriage.com/advice/relationship/using-i-statements-inrelationships/

Johnson, S., & Smith, S. (2023). Unpacking your trust PTSD worksheet patient information section 1: Self-Reflection section 2: Identifying trust deficits section 3: Impact assessment section 4: Goal-setting set realistic and achievable goals for rebuilding trust in yourself, others, and the world. consider both short-term and long-term objectives. https://assets-global.websitefiles.com/600754479f70fb-2c4d356be6/65164e2fcb29002bb158bdb3_Unpacking %20Your%20Trust%20PTSD%20Worksheet%20-%20Sample.pdf

KahaweWithana, S. (2023, January 21). Cognitive distortions and how to overcome them. LinkedIn. https://www.linkedin.com/pulse/cognitive-distortions-howovercomethem-sachintha-kahawewithana-/

Karadeniz, A. (2018, July 23). Cognitive distortions and how to overcome them. Mindunderstanding Itself. https://www.mindunderstandingitself.com/2018/07/23/cognitive-distortionsovercome/

Keohan, E. (2022, September 30). One-Sided relationship: Signs & how to fix it. Talkspace. https://www.talkspace.com/blog/one-sided-relationship/

Kolubinski, D. (2023, August 14). The emotional bank account: Investing in relationships. Reconnect UK. https://www.reconnectuk.com/relationshipenrichment-blog/2023/8/14/the-emotional-bank-account-investing-inrelationships

Krueger, A. (2023, September 1). Trust issues: Signs you have them and how to get over them. Brides. https://www.brides.com/story/signs-trust-issues-hauntingrelationship

Kukde, I. (2022, February 3). 3 side effects of overthinking. PharmEasy Blog. https://pharmeasy.in/blog/overthinking-to-what-extent-can-it-damage-your-life/#Why_overthinking_is_bad

Lachmann, S. (2013, December 24). 10 sources of low self-esteem. Psychology Today. https://www.psychologytoday.com/us/blog/me-we/201312/10-sources-low-selfesteem

Lamothe, C. (2019, October 29). Lack of communication: 17 tips for couples. Healthline. https://www.healthline.com/health/lack-of-communication#communicationtips

Lekkai, F. (2023, June 3). Cognitive distortions: How they affect our mental health. Therasize. https://www.therasize.com/blog/cognitive-distortions-how-theyaffect-our-mental-health

Lewis-Duarte, M. (2021, April 23). Perfectionism is poison; self-compassion is the antidote. Working on Calm. https://workingoncalm.com/perfectionism-and-selfcompassion/

M, J. (2017, August 11). 6 things to consider before investing your emotions into the relationship. Dating International. https://blog.datinginternational.com/investing-your-emotions-intorelationship/

MacLynn, R. V. (2021, August 26). 4 ways perfectionism manifests in a relationship— and how to overcome them. LinkedIn. https://www.linkedin.com/pulse/4-waysperfectionism-manifests-relationshipand-how-rachel-vida/

Markway, B. (2018, December 7). 5 reasons people have low self-confidence. Psychology Today. https://www.psychologytoday.com/us/blog/shyness-is-nice/201812/5reasons-people-have-low-self-confidence

Martin, S. (2019, July 19). Reflective questions to help you quiet your inner perfectionist. Psych Central. https://psychcentral.com/blog/imperfect/2019/07/reflectivequestions-to-help-you-quiet-your-inner-perfectionist#Understand-where-yourperfectionism-comes-from

Matejko , S. (2022, April 26). Perfectionism and anxiety: Why they're linked and ways to cope. Psych Central. https://psychcentral.com/anxiety/perfectionism-andanxiety

McAdam, E. (2021, July 8). Skill #19 how to change how you think: Cognitive distortions part 2 - therapy in a nutshell. Therapy in a Nutshell.

https://therapyinanutshell.com/skill-19-how-to-change-how-you-thinkcognitive-distortions-part-2/

McCallum, K. (2021, April 12). When overthinking becomes a problem & what you can do about it. Houston Methodist.

https://www.houstonmethodist.org/blog/articles/2021/apr/when-overthinking-becomes-a-problem-and-what-you-can-do-aboutit/#:~:text=%22Studies%20show%20that%20ruminating%20on

McDermott, N. (2022, August 25). How to communicate in a relationship, according to experts. Forbes Health. https://www.forbes.com/health/wellness/how-to-communicate-in-a-relationship/

Mead, E. (2019, September 26). What is positive self-talk? Positive Psychology. https://positivepsychology.com/positive-self-talk/

Miles, M. (2022, March 30). Why learning from failure is your key to success. Better Up. https://www.betterup.com/blog/learning-from-failure

Millstein, M. (2021, March 31). Communication studies & corporate communications. Belmont University. https://blogs.belmont.edu/communications/2021/03/31/

Morin, A. (2019a, March 18). Problem-solving is helpful. Overthinking is harmful. Here's how to tell the difference. Inc. https://www.inc.com/amy-morin/problemsolving-is-helpful-overthinking-is-harmful-heres-how-to-tell-difference.html

Morin, A. (2019b, October 15). The difference between helpful problem solving and harmful overthinking. Forbes.

https://www.forbes.com/sites/amymorin/2019/10/15/the-difference-betweenhelpful-problem-solving-and-harmful-overthinking/?sh=41d1bec46e5f

Morin, A. (2023, February 14). How to stop overthinking. Verywell Mind.

https://www.verywellmind.com/how-to-know-when-youre-overthinking5077069

NHS. (2023, April 11). Raising low self-esteem. NHS. https://www.nhs.uk/mental-health/self-help/tips-and-support/raise-low-self-esteem/

Nonis, J. (2023, September 21). 6 shocking effects of emotional suppression and it's hidden consequences . Doug Noll. https://dougnoll.com/emotionalcompetency/emotional-suppression/

Northrup, C., Schwartz, P., & Witte, J. (2014). The normal bar : The surprising secrets of happy couples and what they reveal about creating a new normal in your relationship. Harmony.

Overthinking Disorder: Is It a Mental Illness? (2022, May 16). Cleveland Clinic. https://health.clevelandclinic.org/is-overthinking-a-mental-illness

Pace, R. (2019, August 6). 10 ways to practice self-awareness in relationships. Marriage Advice - Expert Marriage Tips & Advice. https://www.marriage.com/advice/relationship/practicing-self-awareness-inrelationships/

Paige. (2024, March 22). Trust exercises to try with your partner. Love Is Respect. https://www.loveisrespect.org/resources/trust-exercises-to-try-with-yourpartner/

Pattemore , C. (2015, February 25). No rules, just healthy boundaries: Talking relationships. Psych Central. https://psychcentral.com/relationships/whyhealthy-relationships-always-have-boundaries#Healthy-relationship-boundaries

PEAKMD. (2014, January 15). The emotional bank account – A powerful tool in influencing and engaging others. PEAK MD. https://peakmd.ca/the-emotionalbank-account-a-powerful-tool-in-influencing-and-engaging-others/

Perry, E. (2022a, March 30). How to improve self-esteem: 8 tips to give you a boost. BetterUp. https://www.betterup.com/blog/how-to-improve-self-esteem

Perry, E. (2022b, September 14). What is self-awareness and how to develop it. BetterUp. https://www.betterup.com/blog/what-is-self-awareness

Perry, E. (2023, March 14). How to build confidence: A guide to doing it right. BetterUp. https://www.betterup.com/blog/how-to-build-confidence

Plumptre, E. (2023, February 17). Different ways to cope with relationship anxiety. Verywell Mind. https://www.verywellmind.com/learning-how-to-cope-withrelationship-anxiety-5186885

Pollock, D. M. (2023, November 29). Cognitive distortions: What they are, types, and how to manage. Medical News Today.

https://www.medicalnewstoday.com/articles/cognitive-distortions#causes-andtriggers

Powell, A. (2024, March 26). How to stop overthinking in a relationship. Choosing Therapy. https://www.choosingtherapy.com/how-to-stop-overthinking-inrelationships/#:~:text=Practice%20Clear%20Communication,instead%20of%20listening%20to%20respond.&text=It's%20also%20important%20to%20practice, time%20to%20share%20without%20interrupting.

Raypole, C. (2020, November 13). Emotional triggers: Definition and how to manage them. Healthline. https://www.healthline.com/health/mental-health/emotionaltriggers#coping-in-the-moment

Raypole, C. (2021, October 14). One-sided relationship: 14 signs and tips for balance. Healthline. https://www.healthline.com/health/relationships/one-sidedrelationship

Raypole, C., & Pedersen , T. (2021, March 9). The 7 best online couples therapy services in 2023. Psych Central. https://psychcentral.com/reviews/online-couplestherapy#recap

Redhead, S. (2017). Life is a cocktail. Steven Redhead.

Risser, M. (2022, September 15). 13 signs of trust issues & how to get over them. Choosing Therapy. https://www.choosingtherapy.com/trust-issues/

Robbins, T. (2015, December 12). Why your wording matters: Using "I" statements in relationships. Tony Robbins. https://www.tonyrobbins.com/loverelationships/words-matter-you-vs-i/

Saluja, M. (2018, April 16). How to increase your emotional bank account (relationship banking). Body Mind Soul Clinic.

https://www.bodymindsoulclinic.com.au/blog/how-to-increase-your-emotional-bank-account-relationship-banking

Santilli, M. (2022, January 11). What causes overthinking—and 6 ways to stop. Forbes Health. https://www.forbes.com/health/mind/what-causes-overthinking-and-6ways-to-stop/#:~:text=While%20overthinking%20itself%20is%20not

Sarantopoulou, V. (2021, May 2). Overcoming perfectionism in relationships. Anti-Loneliness. https://www.antiloneliness.com/relationships/how-to-overcomeperfectionism-in-your-relationship-5-ways

Schmidt, M. (2020, August 28). How reading fiction increases empathy and encourages understanding. Discover Magazine.
https://www.discovermagazine.com/mind/how-reading-fiction-increasesempathy-and-encourages-understanding

Schmitz, T. (2016, June 3). The importance of emotional awareness in communication. The Conover Company. https://www.conovercompany.com/the-importance-ofemotional-awareness-in-communication/

Scott, E. (2019, May 1). How poor communication causes stress. Lora Hoffstetter.
https://www.hoffstettercounseling.com/post/how-poor-communication-causesstress

Scott, E. (2020, November 25). Improving your communication skills to reduce stress. Verywell Mind. https://www.verywellmind.com/the-stress-of-poorcommunication-with-others-4154175

Scott, E. (2022, January 25). How to improve your relationships with effective communication skills. Verywell Mind.
https://www.verywellmind.com/managing-conflict-in-relationshipscommunication-tips-3144967

Sehat, P. (2023, September 13). The power of I statements: Communicating effectively. Well Beings Counselling. https://wellbeingscounselling.ca/the-power-of-istatements/

Sesha, M. (2019, February 10). 5 reasons people lack self-confidence. Aware - Online Counselling in India. https://awaremh.com/5-reasons-people-lack-selfconfidence/

Sherrell, Z. (2022, January 24). 5 exercises for anxiety. Medical News Today. https://www.medicalnewstoday.com/articles/anxiety-exercises

Simran. (2022, March 15). Difference between anxiety and overthinking. Mantra Care. https://mantracare.org/therapy/what-is/anxiety-and-overthinking/

Sissons, B. (2022, April 26). Low self-esteem and confidence: Signs, causes, and treatment. Medical News Today. https://www.medicalnewstoday.com/articles/ihave-lost-my-confidence-and-self-esteem#causes

Smith, K. (2015, December 10). 7 signs that stress is affecting your relationship. Psych Central. https://psychcentral.com/stress/signs-that-stress-is-affecting-yourrelationship#signs

Smith, S. (2021, June 23). The importance of communication in relationships. Marriage Advice - Expert Marriage Tips & Advice. https://www.marriage.com/advice/communication/importance-ofcommunication-in-relationships/

Star, K. (2020, September 20). How perfectionism can contribute to anxiety. Verywell Mind. https://www.verywellmind.com/perfectionism-and-panic-disorder2584391

10 cognitive distortions that can ruin relationships. (2016, August 20). Psych Central. https://psychcentral.com/blog/10-cognitive-distortions-that-can-ruinrelationships#1

10 ways overthinking ruins relationships. (2018, November 5). Bonobology. https://www.bonobology.com/overthinking-ruins-relationships/

10 ways perfectionism damages relationships and how to overcome it. (2022, May 27). Marriage Advice - Expert Marriage Tips & Advice. https://www.marriage.com/advice/relationship/ways-perfectionism-damagesrelationships/#What_are_some_ways_perfectionism_affects_partnerships

Terzis, G. (2022, August 1). How to escape overthinking and perfectionism - the main causes of analysis paralysis: LinkedIn. https://www.linkedin.com/pulse/howescape-overthinking-perfectionism-main-causes-analysis-terzis/

The importance of communication in a relationship. (2024, February 29). BetterHelp. https://www.betterhelp.com/advice/relations/the-importance-ofcommunication-in-a-relationship/

The importance of self awareness in relationships. (2022, February 28). Perth Counselling and Psychotherapy. https://perthcounsellingandpsychotherapy.com.au/the-importance-of-selfawareness-in-relationships/

The mind maze: How overthinking affects your mental health. (2023, September 14). Strategies for Success. https://www.strategiesforsuccessaz.com/blog/the-mindmaze-how-overthinking-affects-your-mental-health

Understanding fear of intimacy. (2017, March 13). PsychAlive.

https://www.psychalive.org/fear-of-intimacy/

Uniyal, P. (2021, October 22). How overthinking can play havoc with your mental health. Know from an expert. Hindustan Times.

https://www.hindustantimes.com/lifestyle/health/how-overthinking-can-playhavoc-with-your-mental-health-know-from-an-expert-101634882688676.html

Wallbridge, A. (2023, February 27). The importance of self-awareness in emotional intelligence. TSW Training. https://www.tsw.co.uk/blog/leadership-andmanagement/self-awareness-in-emotional-intelligence/

Warren, E. (2023, December 20). Is overthinking the same thing as anxiety? A therapist's take. NOCD. https://www.treatmyocd.com/what-is-ocd/info/relatedsymptoms-conditions/is-overthinking-the-same-thing-as-anxiety-a-therapiststake

Weissberger, T. (2020, September 7). The difference between self confidence and self esteem. ADDA - Attention Deficit Disorder Association. https://add.org/selfconfidence-vs-self-esteem/

Welsh, T. (2023, February 23). How to stop overthinking in a relationship. Thriveworks.

https://thriveworks.com/help-with/relationships/how-to-stop-overthinking-ina-relationship/

What causes low self esteem? (2020, July 28). Advekit.

https://www.advekit.com/blogs/what-causes-low-self-esteem

Wignall, N. (2021, February 17). 7 psychological reasons you overthink everything. Nick Wignall. https://nickwignall.com/7-psychological-reasons-you-overthinkeverything/

Williamson, T. (2013, February 15). 30 questions to ask yourself if you have doubts about your relationship. Tiny Buddha. https://tinybuddha.com/blog/30-questions-tohelp-if-you-have-doubts-about-your-relationship/

Witmer, S. A. (2023, March 24). What is overthinking, and how do I stop overthinking everything? GoodRx. https://www.goodrx.com/health-topic/mental-health/how-can-i-stop-overthinking-everything

Young, K. (2015, May 29). Mindfulness and health: This is why it works. Hey Sigmund. https://www.heysigmund.com/mindfulness-and-health-this-is-why-it-works/

Young, K. (2016, April 11). How anxiety interferes with decision-making - and how to stop it intruding. Hey Sigmund. https://www.heysigmund.com/anxietyinterferes-decision-making-stop-intruding/